Parental Choice

and Education

Parental Choice and Education

PRINCIPLES, POLICY AND PRACTICE

Edited by Mark J Halstead

KOGAN
PAGE

London • Philadelphia

First published in 1994

Apart from any fair dealing for the purposes of research or private study, or criticism
or review, as permitted under the Copyright, Designs and Patents Act, 1988, this
publication may only be reproduced, stored or transmitted, in any form or by any
means, with the prior permission in writing of the publishers, or in the case of
reprographic reproduction in accordance with the terms of licences issued by the
Copyright Licensing Agency. Enquiries concerning reproduction outside those terms
should be sent to the publishers at the undermentioned address:

Kogan Page Limited
120 Pentonville Road
London N1 9JN

British Library Cataloguing in Publication Data

A CIP record for this book is available from the British Library.

ISBN 0 7494 1058 2

Typeset by Books Unlimited (Nottm), Sutton-in-Ashfield, NG17 1AL

Printed and bound in Great Britain by Biddles Ltd, Guildford and King's Lynn

Contents

The Contributors

Brenda Almond is Professor of Moral and Social Philosophy at the University of Hull. She is co-editor of the *Journal of Applied Philosophy* and author of numerous books and articles, including *The Philosophical Quest* (Penguin, 1990), *Moral Concerns* (Humanities Press, 1987) and (as Brenda Cohen) *Education and the Individual* (Allen & Unwin, 1981).

Jean Bendell is currently working in the Department of Child Health at the University of Bristol on a study of language development in twins and closely spaced siblings. As the mother of three home-educated children, she was formerly a county coordinator for 'Education Otherwise', giving advice and support to families considering alternatives in education. She is the author of *School's Out: educating your child at home* (Ashgrove Press, 1987).

Donald Biggs is Professor of Counselling Psychology, Educational Psychology and Religious Studies at the State University of New York at Albany. He is the author of many publications, including (with E G Williamson) *Student Development through Education* (John Wiley, 1975) and (with D Blocher) *Foundations of Ethical Counseling* (Springer, 1987). He has just completed *The Dictionary of Counseling* (Greenwood Press, forthcoming).

Phillip Brown is Lecturer in Sociology at the University of Kent at Canterbury. He previously worked at the Institute of Criminology, Cambridge, and as a craft apprentice at British Leyland, Cowley, Oxford. He has published a number of books, including *Schooling Ordinary Kids* (Tavistock, 1987) and *Degrees of Worth: the Rise of Mass Higher Education and the Decline of Graduate Careers* (with Pat Ainley and Richard Scase, UCL Press, 1994).

Peter Cumper is Lecturer in Law at The Nottingham Trent University. Originally from Northern Ireland, he has also taught at the Universities of Hull and Nottingham. He is particularly interested in human rights and has contributed to a number of law, politics and education journals.

J Mark Halstead is Principal Lecturer in Education at Rolle Faculty of Education, University of Plymouth, and director of the Centre for Research Into Moral, Spiritual and Cultural Understanding and Education (RIMSCUE Centre). He is author of *The Case for Muslim Voluntary-Aided Schools* (Islamic Academy, 1986) and *Education, Justice and Cultural Diversity* (Falmer Press, 1988), and has written articles on educational accountability, children's rights, single-sex schooling, religious and multicultural education and education in Russia.

Terence H McLaughlin is University Lecturer in Education and Fellow of St Edmund's College, Cambridge. He specialises in philosophy of education and has written widely on various aspects of parents' rights in upbringing and education. He is currently secretary of the Philosophy of Education Society of Great Britain and has recently been a visiting scholar in education at Harvard University.

Fred Naylor is Honorary Secretary of The Parental Alliance for Choice in Education (PACE). He was formerly headmaster of the City of Bath Technical College, sixth form curriculum and examinations officer at the Schools Council and lecturer in education at Bath College of Higher Education. He is the author of *Dewsbury: The School above the Pub* (Claridge Press, 1989).

Gerald Porter was awarded his PhD in December 1990 by the State University of New York at Albany, where he is currently Assistant Professor in the Department of Educational Psychology. He has published articles on the psychology of bias and on the role of assessment in home schooling.

Andy Stillman taught for a number of years before joining the National Foundation for Educational Research (NFER). After initial work on test development leading to a PhD, he worked on other research projects, including continuity in education, parental choice of schools and the LEA advisory services, before moving on to become an LEA science inspector. He is the editor of *The Balancing Act of 1980* (NFER, 1986) and co-author of *Choosing Schools* (NFER-Nelson, 1986).

Geoffrey Walford is Senior Lecturer in Sociology and Education Policy at Aston Business School, Aston University. His books include *Life in*

Public Schools (Methuen, 1986), *Restructuring Universities: Politics and Power in the Management of Change* (Routledge, 1987), *Privatization and Privilege in Education* (Routledge, 1990), *City Technology College* (with Henry Miller, Open University Press, 1991) and *Choice and Equity in Education* (Cassell, 1993).

Anne West is Director of Research at the Centre for Educational Research at the London School of Economics and Political Science, having previously been a senior research fellow in the research and statistics branch of the Inner London Education Authority. She has carried out a number of research projects examining choice of schools. She is the author of several articles, chapters and research reports on parental choice in education.

Patricia White is Research Fellow in Philosophy of Education at the University of London Institute of Education. In addition to many papers on ethical and political aspects of philosophy of education, she is the author of *Beyond Domination* (Routledge, 1983), editor of *Personal and Social Education: Philosophical Perspectives* (Kogan Page, 1989) and co-editor with Robin Barrow of *Beyond Liberal Education: Essays in Honour of Paul H Hirst* (Routledge, 1993).

Philip Woods is Research Fellow in the Open University's Centre for Educational Policy and Management and principal investigator for the Parents and School Choice Interaction (PASCI) study. He has written extensively in the past two years on the impact of parental choice on parents and schools. Drawing on his experience as a general manager of the National Confederation of Parent–Teacher Associations and researcher for the National and Welsh Consumer Councils, he has also developed an innovative framework of key relations in education (the concept of the consumer-citizen).

Chapter 1

Parental Choice: An Overview

J Mark Halstead

Whether one sees parental choice in education as simply a fashionable slogan or as a powerful new ideology, its appeal is obvious and compelling. For choice is an expression of autonomy. The *prima facie* virtue of choice in important areas of life, such as marriage, career, domicile, parenthood, and political and religious commitments, is not really open to question. For many, the education of one's children belongs on this list of important areas. The quality of one's life as a parent and indeed as a human being would be diminished without such freedom. Arranged marriages may in fact be just as successful as free-choice marriages, but this does not make them any less abhorrent to most people in the West. The freedom to choose and to take responsibility for one's pathway through life is fundamental.

Two factors complicate the issue, however, in the case of parental choice in education: first, parents are not making a choice on behalf of themselves, but on behalf of other potentially autonomous individuals (their children); and second, the choices that are made impinge directly on the broader society. The first of these factors raises questions about parents' rights and children's rights. Conventional wisdom suggests (a) that parents are in the best position to make decisions about their child's school because they are the ones who know the particular needs and interests of their own child; (b) that there is benefit, especially for the younger child, in attending a school that reflects the values of the child's family; and (c) that parents will increasingly take account of the child's wishes and involve her in the decision-making process as she gets older. Some of these presuppositions are challenged by White in Chapter 6. The second factor raises questions about how far the education of future generations should be a matter for democratic debate by society as a whole, rather than the responsibility of individual parents. Parental choice in education thus involves deeper political and philosophical questions.

Behind the notion of parental choice in education lie three distinct political agendas:

- That of the neo-conservatives, who lament the decline in standards and the loss of traditional authority and who see in educational diversity (which is a prerequisite for real choice) a way of abandoning common schooling and reintroducing selection (Flew, 1987).
- That of the neo-liberals, who favour educational vouchers or other forms of open enrolment. Such market mechanisms are seen as a cost-effective way to improve the educational system without increasing state intervention. Schools which provide what the consumer wants will be rewarded with more enrolments and therefore more income, so that they will thrive, while schools which prove unpopular with the consumer will be forced to improve or else go out of business (Chubb and Moe, 1990).
- That of pluralists, who argue that democratic societies have a duty to avoid assimilationist policies and the imposition of majority values on unwilling minorities or individuals. They wish to see as much variety and flexibility as possible in education in order to be responsive to the needs of individuals and minority groups (Sallis, 1988, p 11). In Denmark, for example, if parents choose not to send their children to the schools provided by the state, they can be paid the money the state saves and can put this towards the fees of any private religious or other school (Hjarnoe, 1993).

These three agendas have little in common beyond their support for parental choice in education. Indeed, they have led to some unexpected alliances, such as the one between British Muslims campaigning for state-funded Muslim schools and right-wing educationalists (see *Islamia*, June 1993, p 3). While some criticisms of parental choice apply equally to all three agendas, others are targeted more specifically at the attack on comprehensive education implicit in the neo-conservative approach, for example, or at the concept of democracy which underpins the pluralist approach.

General criticisms of the notion of parental choice in education fall into two main categories: those to do with social justice, and those to do with efficiency and practicability.

The criticisms relating to issues of social justice involve two possible outcomes from a policy of choice. First, the choices made by individual parents may not coincide with the needs of society as a whole. Parents may select schools, for example, which do little to encourage children's sense of citizenship or they may choose schools in a way which leads directly or indirectly to increased racial segregation (see Chapter 12). The danger that any form of racial separatism would seriously threaten the stability and cohesion of society as a whole forms the basis for the Swann Report's rejection of Muslim voluntary-aided schools (see Halstead, 1986). Second, the choices made by parents are likely to widen existing inequalities in schools by serving first and foremost the needs of the articulate, well-informed middle classes who insist on 'obtaining the "best buy" for their children' (Jonathan, 1989, p 323). Ball argues that market mechanisms will lead schools to welcome more able students (in order to ensure good 'performance outcomes') and turn away students 'with expensive learning needs' (such as excluded students, those for whom English is a second language or those with special educational needs) in order to 'maximise the impact of resources on outcomes' (1993, p 7). The latter are then likely to be left with no choice other than the less popular and therefore less well funded and less well resourced schools, so that their initial disadvantage is reinforced. Recent reports from Bradford suggest that working class Asian parents living in inner-city districts are much less successful than any other group in getting the school of their choice (Chaudhary, 1993). Drawing on evidence from a decade of open enrolment in Scotland, Adler concludes that although there have been gainers as well as losers from the introduction of open enrolment, the balance sheet suggests that parental choice 'has been a "negative sum game" in which the gains achieved by some pupils have been more than offset by the losses incurred by others and by the community as a whole' (1993, p 3).

Other criticisms relate to questions about the efficiency and practicability of any system of parental choice. Unpopular schools may end up offering an even worse education than before because of reduced funding, while popular schools are likely to receive more applications than they have places. The inevitable result is that the latter schools will have to apply some form of selection procedure, and some parents, through no fault of their own, will not get what they choose.

The problem is that schools are not a true market situation (Sallis, 1988, Ch 2). First, there are limits to their capacity to expand to take account of increased consumer demand. Second, the government is seeking to define the criteria by which schools are judged (by league tables of examination results, for example, and inspectors' reports) rather than leave these to the consumer. Third, education is not a commodity, nor are growth, competition and financial success necessarily marks of a good school. There is a real anxiety that educational values might lose their primacy in any market-directed educational reforms. Even O'Hear, on balance a supporter of the free-market approach to education, concedes that 'we must look outside the market for institutions to uphold morality and taste' (1991, p 37).

For some, as we have seen, it is diversity in educational provision which is the key to the debate. Until recently, the main choices open to parents – if, indeed, they had any choice at all – lay between private and maintained education (see Johnson, 1990) and between church and non-church schools (see Rogers, 1982). In addition, of course, parents have had a more fundamental choice – whether to send their children to school or to educate them at home (see Chapter 11). The present Conservative administration in Britain is committed both to increasing the number of options available and to extending the possibility of choice to more people. This policy involves the creation of new kinds of school, both as a result of government initiatives (city technical colleges and grant maintained schools) and by allowing independent religious and other schools to opt into the state system of education. A certain amount of selection and specialisation will be allowed in some of these new schools. A halt to the policy of abandoning single-sex education will increase the reality of choice for some groups (Halstead, 1991). The possibility of other kinds of schooling, such as mini-schools, small schools and flexi-schools looms on the horizon, if Britain continues to follow American initiatives (Meighan and Toogood, 1992). The cumulative effect of such diversification should be that many parents will in fact be able to choose among schools with a different ethos and with different academic emphases, though not, of course, a different basic curriculum (except by going outside the state-funded system). However, the research findings of Fitz, Halpin and Power (1993) suggest that government initiatives such as grant-maintained status have not done much so far to help foster diversity and increase parental choice.

An important outcome of any parental choice policy is the increase in information offered to parents, particularly in school prospectuses and governors' reports (Advisory Centre for Education, 1992). Ostensibly this is to facilitate the exercise of informed consumer choice, but it is also likely to have the effect of increasing schools' accountability. There has been a gradual shift in recent years from approaches to accountability based on the professional autonomy of teachers to approaches based on consumerism (Halstead, 1994). Johnson suggests that a policy of parental choice might result in clearer aims for individual institutions and greater respect for the client by professionals as well as in greater commitment by parents to the schools their children attend and to the educational process generally (1990, pp 140–145).

From what has been said so far, it is clear that the topic of parental choice is capable of inspiring deep disagreements at a level of both principle and policy. The aim of the present volume is in no way to present a particular party line, but rather to open up the debate and explore the issues by bringing together authors with a wide range of political and other commitments as well as others who wish to refrain from revealing their personal perspectives. The intention is that by the juxtaposition of different viewpoints the reader will be put in a position to evaluate the arguments and views directly, rather than be faced with, as it were, a secondhand exposition of them in a volume written from a single viewpoint. In addition to the ideological diversity in the book, the authors are writing from the standpoint of different disciplines, including history, philosophy, sociology and law. In the overall balance of the book, therefore, the reader will be introduced not only to the key topics within the debate about parental choice, but also to its complexity and to the sheer variety of possible perspectives, interests and commitments.

In Chapter 2, Stillman provides an overview of the historical development of parental choice in Britain during the last 50 years and shows that many of the current issues and conflicts can only be understood by reference to earlier policy. Perhaps more than any other area of educational policy, parental choice in Britain has been clearly influenced by developments in the USA (Bondi, 1991; Edwards and Whitty, 1992). In Chapter 3, Biggs and Porter review the growth of interest in parental choice in the USA and describe some of the main initiatives. One interesting finding is that such initiatives have much more frequently resulted from a desire to meet the needs of underachieving pupils than have similar policies in the UK.

Chapter 4 marks a significant attempt to develop a theory of parental choice. Writing from a sociological perspective, Brown argues that the shift from an ideology of meritocracy (in which educational decisions are based on the abilities and efforts of pupils) to an ideology of 'parentocracy' (in which educational decisions are based on the wishes and influence of parents) marks a new stage in educational provision. He examines the causes of this shift and its implications for our understanding of the relationship between education, the family and the state.

The next three chapters address the philosophical debate about parental choice. In Chapter 5, Almond refers to the conflict between the state, parents and professionals as to who represents children. Conventions on human rights give priority to parents in education, but modern states tend to make uniform provision, leaning towards a monopoly position. She argues that liberty is best preserved if the conflict is resolved in favour of parents for (a) only parental decision-making guarantees educational variety and change; (b) the parental relationship itself generates rights, including one derived from the broader political right to cultural and religious freedom; and (c) the beneficial operation of market forces in education depends upon leaving power of decision-making in the hands of parents. In Chapter 6, White argues that in a democratic plural society parents do not have rights *qua* parents over the education of their children, but they do have educational responsibilities, and she suggests that a partnership between parents and schools offering a common civic education is the most appropriate way forward. In Chapter 7, McLaughlin further explores some philosophical aspects of the contrasting views of parental rights contained in Chapters 5 and 6, and draws attention to the complexity of some of the questions at issue.

The next two chapters review the findings of recent empirical research. West in Chapter 8 examines the factors that influence parents' choice of primary, secondary and private schools, including the part played by pupils themselves in the choice. Woods in Chapter 9 outlines some of the ways in which schools are adapting and responding to the quasi-market; the chapter highlights the danger of over-reliance on choice as a lever of change and the strength of collaborative responses through schools working together.

In Chapter 10, Walford distinguishes 'weak' choice (ie the expression of a preference among existing state-funded schools) from the 'strong' choice with which this chapter and the next are concerned, in which families help to shape the choices on offer. Walford's chapter describes a group of private evangelical Christian schools and outlines the reasons why parents and others feel the need to start such schools. Similarly, Bendell in Chapter 11 examines the legal right of parents to educate their children at home and the reasons why significant numbers of parents take this path.

Writing from a legal perspective, Cumper in Chapter 12 addresses the possibility that increased parental choice and diversity of schooling might exacerbate racial divisions in society, especially in the aftermath of the Carney case in Cleveland. Finally, in Chapter 13, Naylor describes some of the cases in which the Parental Alliance for Choice in Education has been involved. In sketching the philosophy of this pressure group, he offers a spirited restatement of many of the arguments of the neo-conservatives in support of parental choice.

References

Adler, M (1993) *An Alternative Approach to Parental Choice* (Briefing no 13) London, National Commission on Education.

Advisory Centre for Education (1992) *Bulletin 48* (July–August) London, ACE.

Ball, S J (1993) 'Education markets, choice and social class: the market as a class strategy in the UK and the USA' *British Journal of Sociology of Education*, 14, 1, pp 3–19.

Bondi, L (1991) 'Choice and diversity in school education: comparing developments in the United Kingdom and the USA' *Comparative Education*, 27, 2, pp 125–34.

Chaudhary, V (1993) 'Parents claim racism in school choice policy' *The Guardian*, 26 July, p 2.

Chubb, J and Moe, T (1990) *Politics, Markets and America's Schools* Washington DC, Brookings Institution.

Edwards, A and Whitty G (1992) 'Parental choice and educational reform in Britain and the United States' *British Journal of Educational Studies*, 40, 2, pp 101–17.

Fitz, J, Halpin, D and Power, S (1993) *Grant-maintained Schools: Education in the Market-place* London, Kogan Page.

Flew, A (1987) *Power to the Parents* London, Sherwood Press.

Halstead, J M (1986) *The Case for Muslim Voluntary Aided Schools: Some Philosophical Reflections* Cambridge, Islamic Academy.

Halstead, J M (1991) 'Radical feminism, Islam and the single sex school debate' *Gender and Education*, 3, 3, pp 263–78.

Halstead, J M (1994) 'Accountability and values' in Scott, D (ed) *Accountability and Control in Educational Settings* London, Cassell.

Hjarnoe, J (1993) *Islamic Schools in Denmark* Paper presented to an international conference at the University of Oxford School of Geography, 5–7 April.

Johnson, D (1990) *Parental Choice in Education* London, Unwin Hyman.

Jonathan, R (1989) 'Choice and control in education: parental rights, individual liberties and social justice' *British Journal of Educational Studies*, 37, 4, pp 321–38.

Meighan, R and Toogood, P (1992) *Anatomy of Choice in Education* Ticknall, Education Now.

O'Hear, A (1991) *Education and Democracy: Against the Educational Establishment* London, Claridge Press.

Rogers, R (1982) 'Church Schools' *Where?* (June), pp 6–13.

Sallis, J (1988) *Schools, Parents and Governors* London, Routledge.

Chapter 2

Half a Century of Parental Choice in Britain?

Andy Stillman

Much of what we now know as 'parental choice' in Britain can be traced back to 1943 and the writing of the 1944 Education Act. Perhaps the most important lesson that can be learnt from looking back over these years is that parental choice of school is a difficult idea to implement. This is hardly surprising, since on the small scale one person's choice in a finite system can so easily bring about another's denial. On the larger scale, choice typifies the conflict between the wants of the individual and the needs of the group.

While both the thinking about and the implementation of choice may have advanced over recent years, it has been a tortuous process and one that has developed a number of seemingly inescapable tensions and conflicts. The identification of these often emotive factors or conflicts can help us understand the development of choice as an idea over the years and how we have reached the current position. The main conflicts are set out as follows:

- Choice necessitates spare places, but spare places cost money.
- Parents might wish to choose a school that for selective reasons or reasons of distance is not open to their child; in some areas only the ability to pay for transport opens access to choice.
- Choice for some parents can reduce choice for others.
- Choice requires educational diversity between schools, so that there is something to choose between other than simply good and bad (for that is no choice); the central control involved in the development of the National Curriculum appears to conflict with this principle.

- To make informed choices, parents need an appropriate level of information and interest, especially if the purpose of choice is to improve education, but research suggests that children may in fact be making the decisions as much as parents (see Chapter 8).

- Central government appears to be using the rhetoric of parental choice as part of its drive to reduce the educational management carried out by Local Education Authorities (LEAs) and to substitute strong central control in tandem with small-scale local control through governing bodies; Lawlor (1988), for example, expresses the view that the dominance of LEAs in the running of schools is one of the most serious threats to education reform.

These conflicts and difficulties have emerged over the years and are still evident in the situation today. When *The Parents' Charter* (Department of Education and Science, 1991) advocates the advantages of choice, but in doing so still has to give similar caveats to those that first appeared in 1943, one might question just how much extra choice has really been gained:

> You have a duty to ensure that your child gets an education – and you can choose the school that you would like your child to go to. Your choice is wider as a result of recent changes ... You have a right to a place in the school you want unless it is full to capacity with pupils who have a stronger claim ... Selective grammar schools can keep empty places if not enough pupils pass their selection tests. (pp 9–10)

Similarly, the inherent difficulties in linking choice with the improvement of standards and the provision of diversity can still be seen in *Choice and Diversity* (Department for Education, 1992) where the foreword and conclusion contain seeming contradictions. In looking at the progress of parental choice, it is also worth following the progress of these issues and conflicts.

The 1943 Education Bill and the 1944 Education Act

Although a number of ideas about parental choice had arisen prior to the writing of the 1944 Education Act, much of current thinking and practice stems from this point. Most significant, perhaps, is Section 76 of the 1944 Education Act:

> The Minister and local education authorities shall have regard to the general principle that, so far as is compatible with the provision of efficient instruction and training and the avoidance of unreasonable public expenditure, pupils are to be educated in accordance with the wishes of their parents.

Perhaps surprisingly, however, the idea of parental choice between *like* schools was never its main purpose. In fact, parents' wishes were not mentioned at all in the original White Paper, *Educational Reconstruction* (Board of Education, 1943), nor in the 1943 Bill itself. This part of the Bill was concerned with bringing denominational schools into the state system and ensuring that parents could still opt for the school of their faith.

The duty to accede to parents' wishes wherever possible was introduced during the debate stages as one of the general duties upon LEAs. Although it was not phrased in denominational terms, the Earl of Selborne's comment that failure to fulfil this duty would be a 'form of religious intolerance' makes the context very clear (HL Committee, Vol 132, Col 287, 20 June 1944). Some three weeks later, this initial duty to parents was rephrased to become a 'General Principle'. As Section 76 of the Act, it explicitly laid the foundations for parental choice of school but implicitly still only referred to a denominational choice. In the context of that time a denominational rider would have been superfluous.

The Development of Parental Choice 1944–1976

At first, the issue of parental choice in school allocation aroused little concern, although a small number of admissions appeals and complaints did go forward to the Minister based upon Sections 68 and 37 of the Act. The main problem with these was that time-consuming decisions had to be made interpreting the woolly areas of 'unreasonableness' and 'unsuitability'. There was also another problem. Section 37 of the Act, by chance, gave the parents' arguments more strength than they had initially had under Section 76. Under

Section 37, the parents' choice of school had to be accepted unless the LEA could give good reason to refute it. Under Section 68, the procedure was the other way around.

In 1946, the Ministry of Education issued Circular 83, *Choice of Schools*, to clarify the issues surrounding parents' and LEAs' rights. The aim does not seem to have been to alter the amount of 'parental choice' so much as to let local authorities know what guidelines the Minister would use when faced with appeals. It was hoped that these guidelines would reduce the mismatch between LEA and ministry decisions and thus reduce the amount of administrative work done by the Minister with central (as opposed to local) appeals from parents.

Circular 83 was principally concerned with choice based on selection, denomination, or ease of access. The idea of choice between *like* schools (ie between schools of a similar organisation, type or status) had yet really to be acknowledged, though the Circular did offer a fourth, and somewhat ambiguous, reason for choice: educational considerations. This might involve the choice of a particular school because it provided a particular type of advanced work. The 1944 Act had, of course, set up a variety of types of specialist schools to choose from.

The implicit assumption that choice between like schools was of little importance was even more evident when the Minister commented on primary schools:

> In the case of primary education the question of selecting a school of a particular educational type does not arise ... parents generally may be expected to select the school of the appropriate age range most convenient to their homes. (Ministry of Education, 1946)

Four years later, the Labour government's Ministry of Education published its 'Manual of Guidance: Schools, No.1', which was again entitled *Choice of Schools*. This opened up the range of legitimate grounds for choice of school. Thus, while it began with a qualification: 'At the onset it should be noted that Section 76 does not confer on the parent complete freedom of choice', on the very next page it stated: 'Section 76 is not limited to choices made on denominational grounds. Nor does it apply merely to the initial choice of a school.'

The Manual offered three 'strong' reasons parents could give when choosing an alternative school and a further five which an LEA could properly take into account:

- denominational reasons;
- educational reasons (provision of a particular type of work in a particular school);
- linguistic reasons (ie use of Welsh or English);
- convenience of access;
- special facilities at a school (for example, provision of midday meals, thus allowing parents to work all day);
- · preference for a single-sex or mixed school;
- family association with a particular school;
- medical reasons.

While increasing the number of permissible reasons for choice, the government also saw fit to strengthen the administrative arguments against it. Acceptable reasons for refusing parental choice included:

- overcrowding and 'zoning';
- attendance at all-age, unreorganised schools;
- avoidance of unreasonable public expenditure;
- extra-district charges;
- transport costs and time of journey.

In this document we see one of the first overt references to the idea of there being a 'balance':

> The practical problem of administration, therefore, which faces local education authorities, is how far effect should be given to the parents' wishes ... Some of the relevant considerations (ie the strengths of the parents' and LEA's arguments) ... may need to be balanced against each other before a decision is reached. (Ministry of Education, 1950)

Many of the arguments both for and against acceding to choice are clearly still recognisable today, though the balance in the 1950s would appear to have favoured the LEA's management of its resources a little more.

There was little change on the parental choice front over the next 20 years. In other areas, though, there were significant developments, especially in respect of the comprehensive ideal. This advanced as an idea in the 1950s but had to wait until the return of Labour to office in 1964 before it was set in motion with Circular 10/65 (Department of Education and Science, 1965). However, neither the supporting legislation nor Labour's 1970 Education Green Paper saw the light of day before the Conservatives regained office in 1970. Among other proposals in this unpublished Green Paper were plans for stronger rights for parents, independent appeals, easier transfers and parental participation on governing bodies (*The Times*, 25 March 1969). Some of these ideas reappeared two years later, albeit somewhat abridged, in *Labour's Programme for Britain* (Labour Party, 1972).

The Conservative government of 1970–74 maintained an anti-comprehensive stance in public but recognised that not all Conservative councils shared this view. As demonstrated in the February 1974 Conservative Manifesto (Conservative Party, 1974a), this government saw the wishes of parents as having four elements:

- the parents' choice of type of state school system (comprehensive or selective, mixed or single-sex) for their locality and thus, implicitly, for their child;
- the parents' choice between the independent or state sectors;
- the parents' choice of denominational or non-denominational schools;
- (still somewhat masked) the parents' choice between like state schools.

The First Parents' Charter

In February 1974, the Conservatives lost the election and soon after, in October 1974, were faced with another. The change in education policy between these two elections was considerable: the attack on comprehensive education was toned down and in its place an appeal to parents' 'rights' was brought forward, based, in part, upon the view that comprehensive education represented a possible denial of these 'rights'. The Conservative Party Manifesto for October 1974 explained this new parents' charter:

An important part of the distinct Conservative policy on education is to recognise parental rights. A say in how their children are to be brought up is an essential ingredient in the parental role. We will therefore introduce additional rights for parents. First, by amending the 1944 Education Act, we will impose clear obligations on the state and local authorities to take account of the wishes of parents. Second, we will consider establishing a local appeal system for parents dissatisfied with the allotment of schools. Third, parents will be given the right to be represented on school boards by requiring a substantial proportion of the school governors and managers to be drawn from, and elected by, the parents of children currently at school. Fourth, we will place an obligation on all head teachers to form a parent-teachers association to assist and support teachers. Fifth, we will encourage schools to publish prospectuses about their record, existing character, specialities and objectives. (Conservative Party, 1974b)

The charter can thus be seen to have developed out of earlier ideas, some of which were very similar to those in Labour's unpublished 1970 Green Paper, and to have overtly sown the seeds for future legislation. At the time, however, it was just one of a broad tranche of similar individual rights policies that were being proposed, many of which have since died.

Discussion of parental choice or even power in educational decision-making appeared regularly in parliamentary debates in the mid-1970s with strong pressure for the legislation to tilt the balance slightly towards the parents. The idea of local appeal committees was further considered and it was suggested that in local appeals, LEAs should have to prove why choice should *not* be given rather than parents having to prove why it should. In future, it was argued, the norm should be that children should be educated in accordance with the wishes of the parents unless it could be shown positively by the LEA that it was unreasonable to do so on the ground of the cost involved. This idea was, in effect, anticipating the important 1984 *South Glamorgan* High Court judgment by some nine years (see page 186). The need for diversity of provision if choice was to be real was also discussed at this stage. The Parents' Charter Bill, as a Private Member's Bill, was talked out of the Commons and never became law.

The Voucher as a means to Choice

Ideas about vouchers had been around for many years when they resurfaced in 1974–75. The Conservative MP, Dr Rhodes Boyson believed that the introduction of vouchers, redeemable at either private or state schools, would transform the educational scene with improved diversity and increased parental involvement. On the Labour side, vouchers were regarded with abhorrence. Ernest Armstrong, Labour Parliamentary Under-Secretary for Education, commented:

> We have to face reality, which is that up to 85 per cent of our children will have no choice at all. The voucher system is seen by the Government as being socially divisive. On principle we are against it ... Education is not to be sold across the counter like groceries. It is far more important. (HC Oral Questions, Vol 891, Col 1202, 6 May 1975)

In 1975, Kent County Council commissioned a feasibility study into the use of vouchers which suggested that they would be impractical (Kent County Council, 1978). Kent later attempted a further experiment with the less ambitious idea of 'open enrolment'. This again showed that the realisation of parental choice created problems with the operating of schools and was too expensive within a state system which had to provide for all. The problem was that Kent parents, not unreasonably, would not choose in such a way that most schools could be equally full, with the rest being completely emptied. In practice some schools needed extra classrooms while others, with reduced intakes, still had to be kept open to satisfy a diminished but still significant, local demand. *The Guardian* commented that it was difficult to imagine a more expensive way of managing schools (12 August 1983).

The Appeal System

Up to 1976, most parental allocation complaints and appeals to Ministers and then Secretaries of State for Education had been based upon Section 68 of the 1944 Act, with only a few based upon Section 37(3), the School Attendance Order which required the child to be kept out of school before it could be enacted. As described earlier, both sections required the Secretary of State to interpret woolly terminology. Legislating to interpret reasonableness under Section 68 had proved difficult for the Labour government, but the Tameside court judgment in 1976 offered a definitive interpretation. This suggested that the

Secretary of State could no longer be satisfied that an authority was acting or proposing to act unreasonably unless no reasonable authority could ever act in that way (see Fowler, 1979; Bull, 1987). Over the following years there were very few instances of a Secretary of State giving directions to an LEA concerning allocations under Section 68 (Bull, 1985). Section 37 appeals were unaffected by this judgment and continued to be the easier path for parents to take.

In the late 1960s and 1970s the number of central appeals (there were few local appeals to speak of then) grew dramatically, from about 100 per year prior to comprehensive reorganisation, to around 1,000 or more per year in the early 1970s (Department of Education and Science, 1977). For all the large number, the parents' success rate was very low; for example, in 1977, only two out of 1,124 Section 68 complaints and only 24 out of 40 Section 37 appeals were upheld. However, this large number of appeals was becoming a problem for the government. It was time-consuming and politically messy. Something had to be done, and the response to this problem led directly to the 1977 and 1979 White Papers and the 1980 Education Act (Meredith, 1981; Newell, 1983; Passmore, 1983).

The 1977 White Paper

The Labour government in 1976–77 had to respond to three recognisable pressures: a perceived growing demand for parental choice; imminent falling rolls at a time of economic difficulty; and the embarrassing problem of appeals. The 1977 Consultation Paper, *Admission of Children to Schools of their Parents' Choice* (Department of Education and Science, 1977), presented Shirley Williams' solutions to all three points. Amongst other things, it suggested that:

1. Parental preference should be regarded as having a degree of intrinsic validity and must be given a channel of expression that allows it to be taken into account together with other factors from the outset of the allocation procedure.
2. LEAs should be able to plan the operating capacity of their schools and to refuse a child a place at a particular school (unless there are special reasons to the contrary) if the school is full to that capacity.
3. Each authority's arrangements should also include a procedure for

local appeals. Normally (ie when this operated) the Secretary of State would not consider a complaint from a parent until the case had been considered on appeal. Section 37(3) of the 1944 Act would be repealed and consequential amendments made to Section 37(4). Questions of admissions to schools would be specifically excluded from consideration under Section 68.

Shirley Williams has subsequently argued that these proposals would have moved the balance towards the parents (Williams, 1985). Others may see it differently, however, since the arguments emphasising the LEAs' management role and allowing them to block choice were also strengthened. It was suggested that LEAs could block choice if acceding to it would

- breach the planned operating capacity as determined by the LEA;
- have adverse affects on the efficient provision of education in the school or in the area, or conflict with the comprehensive principle as described in Section 1 of the Education Act 1976;
- produce a conflict if the school was unsuitable to the age, ability or aptitude of the child.

The parents' redress to appeal was also to be weakened. The Secretary of State proposed that 'appeals' should be LEA reviews of LEA decisions and that she should only be brought in on procedural matters. Labour's 1977 response to the Parents' Charter was, in essence, a management charter.

For the most part, these recommendations appeared in similar form a year later in the 1978 Education Bill. This failed to reach the statute books, however, as the Labour government went to the polls too soon for the Bill to get through Parliament and a Conservative government took up power in 1979.

The 1980 Education Act

The new Conservative government brought in two Education Acts in quick succession. The first, in 1979, simply served to overturn the 1976 Education Act and to remove the element in it of compulsory comprehensive reorganisation. The second, the 1980 Education Act, contained many elements of Labour's 1978 Bill but shifted the balance once more towards the parents, in line with Conservative philosophy. That the Act is so similar to the 1978 Bill is really not surprising since the three major problems facing the previous government were still there.

Some within the Tory party wanted to move the balance towards the parents even further. For example, they asked whether there was any need for admissions limits. Could not the system operate perfectly well on market forces alone? If there needed to be a curb, could it not be based solely upon the efficient provision and cost of resources argument? In the end the Secretary of State upheld the use of a guide figure, the 'intended intake', but he gave it no force of law in its own right. He simply required it to be published for parents' information.

However, the Act still permitted an LEA not to comply with parental preference if the preference would:

- prejudice the provision of efficient education or the efficient use of resources;
- clash with the principles of a voluntary aided or special agreement school; or
- clash with selective principles.

In Circular 1/81, the Department of Education and Science (DES) suggested that the intended intake figure should 'be the number beyond which the authority or governors would normally refuse to make further admissions to the school' (DES, 1981a). Thus, if an LEA tied the intended intake to the first reason above, the figure would effectively become the maximum intake for efficiency (so to speak) and could therefore ride with the legal status of the efficient education and resources argument.

The 1980 Act allowed for a certain amount of LEA autonomy in defining 'efficient education or the efficient use of resources'. But many Conservatives were unsure about giving LEAs unlimited power to decide on parental rights and it was felt that some form of local appeal should be instigated to act as a balance between parents and LEAs. Local appeal committees were thus set up principally to decide between individual parents and the LEA. It was also felt that in doing this the appeal committees would have a positive influence on those initially making the allocation decisions. Contrary to expectation, however, the appeal committees were not intended to be independent. Dr Rhodes Boyson argued that since LEA representatives were in the majority on the appeal committees, he would be surprised if

> the appeal tribunal were to create a vast problem for itself by putting 200 more children into a school where there was no room for them ... It would be a funny local authority which set up all kinds of appeal tribunals which were in constant battle with the local authority. (Boyson, HC Debate, Education (No 2) Bill Standing Committee D, Cols 552 and 630)

Clearly, the 1980 Education Act attempted to move the balance towards the parents but the final decision lay with the appeal committees which appear to have been asked to play contradictory roles. Their pro-parent role must be set against their composition which gave them a majority of LEA or voluntary aided school appointees. Further, the appeal committees had to take the LEAs' or schools' published admissions arrangements into account.

The application of a statutory local appeals procedure to the LEAs' allocation procedures was new to the education system in 1982 although many LEAs had run their own appeals system beforehand. Numbers of appeals reached 10,000 by 1983 and have risen ever since. Quite what is gained by all this appealing must also be questionable: arbitration between the parents and the LEA is bound to result in many unsatisfied customers, particularly since, if the LEA has done its job properly, there should be no places left in the schools according to the LEA's definition. How then can a committee ever satisfy a parent's appeal without challenging or even changing the LEA's arguments? Furthermore, unless more children are actually squeezed into the popular schools (thus possibly reducing their effectiveness and popularity) appeal committees cannot actually generate more choice – they simply arbitrate over who gains access to the places available. The increasing number of appeals demonstrates increasing *expectations* of choice rather than an increasing *amount* of choice. With more appeals there will be more refusals, and hence more frustration.

It should be noted, however, that Section 68 appeals to the Minister still exist. The 1980 Act set out to reduce central appeals on matters of allocation, particularly by re-routing Section 37 appeals back to the local appeal committee, but Section 68 was not repealed. In 1982, there were approximately 300 complaints to the Secretary of State under this section, and, although none of them was upheld, the problem has not really gone away (Newell, 1983; cf Stillman and Maychell, 1986).

As with the 1978 Education Bill, the 1980 Act had strong management overtones but there were also claims that through its emphasis on choice the Act would bring about improved parental involvement (St John Stevas, 1977; Atherton, 1979) and indeed, better schooling (Sugarman, 1979; Joseph, 1982).

Developments in Parental Choice 1980-93

The 1980 Act has been heralded as representing the first part of a 13-year initiative by the Conservative government to increase parental choice and raise standards in education. It is claimed that the 1993 Education Bill (and eventually Act) represents the culmination of this process (Department for Education, 1992).

This initiative has involved at least 12 Education Acts as well as the 1993 Bill (see *The Observer*, 1993, p 17). Several of these Acts have been particularly relevant to the issues of choice:

- The 1980 Education Act (see above).
- The 1986 Education (No 2) Act, which required governors to provide more information for parents, including the introduction of the Annual Parents' Meeting.
- The 1988 Education Act, which brought in the National Curriculum, local management of schools (LMS), grant-maintained schools, city technical colleges and a relaxation of admission limits to give 'open enrolment'.
- The 1992 Schools Act, which brought in annual reports to parents on pupils' performance, the requirement for LEAs to produce league tables of exam results and other performance indicators, and the requirement for governors to provide more data in their reports to parents. This Act also brought in the Office for Standards in Education (OFSTED) and the new system of inspection.

Throughout this period, the government claims to have continued to pursue and develop a number of significant themes, in particular, quality, diversity, increasing parental choice, greater autonomy for schools, and greater accountability, though it is arguable as to whether the combination of the last four of these elements will enhance the first, and indeed how far any of the legislation has actually increased choice.

Patently, elements within this legislation need teasing out in more detail. For instance, the continuing appeal to parents as consumers can only work where there is choice. The main effect of much of this legislation will be to change the procedures for deciding which parents have access to which schools and to shift the control of that access from LEA officer to appeals committee. Clearly, access to a more or less fixed number of places still has to be decided by a particular set of criteria. Thus if one system is changed for another, a different set of parents may gain the priority access.

For a Conservative government, the ideas of parental choice and diversity of provision are further enhanced by the assisted places scheme whereby financial help is given for a number of children to attend independent schools (Section 17 of the 1980 Act). By 1984/85 the number of 'assisted pupils' had risen to 17,336, which represented an estimated 0.25 per cent of the maintained school population (*Education*, 'Parliament', 12 July 1985.) This figure has subsequently risen and represents a significant part of the income of the country's independent schools; 26,740 children had assisted places in 1990/91; 27,641 children in 1991/92; and 28,674 in 1992/93. For 1991/92, the assisted places scheme cost £78,875,000 (Department for Education, private communication, July 1993).

As part of the same move to offer greater diversity of provision (as well as being concerned with wresting control of schools from LEAs), the government brought in city technology colleges (CTCs) and grant maintained status (GMS) in the 1988 Education Act. However, the number of CTC places currently available is so small as to not change the global amount of parental choice available, and new research has shown that GM schools have not actually provided new alternatives or offered wider choice (Fitz, Power and Halpin, 1993). In an OFSTED report in April 1993, teaching standards and examination performance in GM Schools were shown to be little different from the norm. One might well wonder if the current political effort might not be greater than the corresponding effect, though with more schools being attracted to seek grant maintained status for straightforward financial gain, the numbers of schools left working with their LEAs is certainly diminishing.

Clearly, however, whatever else it has done, the legislation has enhanced the quantity of information available to parents, a trend which has accompanied all proposals since 1974. Current requirements include the publication of examination and Standard Assessment Task (SAT) results, the demand for league tables, 'truancy' rates, inspection reports, and governors' reports to parents (with their associated meetings). But there may be a confusion here between the provision of information for the purposes of accountability, and the provision of information to enable parents to make informed choices.

A perhaps surprising anomaly is that parents as a whole do not seem to be searching for more information. Attendance at governors' parents' meetings is consistently low, even in schools which otherwise attract good parental involvement. A recent survey in Bradford indicated that the majority of parents were against the publication of league tables (*Times Educational Supplement*, 30 April 1993, p 2). These results supported similar findings from Scotland (ibid).

Where then have 50 years of expensive parental choice initiatives taken us? At the outset one should acknowledge that parents now have more opportunities to express a choice than before, more expectations of taking an active interest in their children's education and more bits of almost comparable information to help them make their choice. Whether the information is precisely what is needed is less certain, however, when so much research suggests that it is the children that really make the choice and that for entry to secondary school they do so two or three years before transfer (Stillman and Maychell, 1986; Thomas and Dennison, 1991). As to the potential diversity, it is true there are more non-LEA schools than before, and CTCs have industrial sponsorship, but so far what outcome has there been from any of this except to drain funds away from other schools? In any case, any increase in diversity of provision has to be set against the restrictions imposed by the same government by the introduction of the National Curriculum and its testing.

What is certain is that the issue will run for a good while yet and that whatever may currently be thought about the 1993 Education Bill ending 13 years of change and development, there is undoubtedly more to come.

References

Atherton, G (1979) *Reaching Out to Parents* Glasgow, Scottish Consumer Council.

Board of Education (1943) *Educational Reconstruction*, Cmd 6458, London, HMSO.

Bull, D (1985) 'Monitoring education appeals: local ombudsmen lead the way' *Journal of Social Welfare Law*, July, pp 184–226.

Bull, D (1987) 'Tameside: prospectively "reasonable"; retrospectively "Maladministration"' *Modern Law Review*, 50 (May), pp 307–44.

Conservative Party (1974a) *Firm Action for a Fair Britain* (The Conservative Manifesto) London, Conservative Central Office.

Conservative Party (1974b) *Putting Britain First: A National Policy from the Conservatives* London, Conservative Central Office.

Department of Education and Science (1965) *Circular 10/65* London, HMSO.

Department of Education and Science (1977) *Admission of Children to Schools of Their Parents' Choice* London, DES.

Department of Education and Science (1981) *Circular 1/81 Education Act 1980 Admission to Schools* London, DES.

Department of Education and Science (1991) *The Parents' Charter: You and Your Child's Education*, London, DES.

Department for Education (1992) *Choice and Diversity – A New Framework for Schools* London, HMSO.

Fitz, J, Power, S and Halpin, D (1993) 'Opting for grant maintained status' *Policy Studies Journal*, Spring.

Fowler, G (1979) 'The accountability of ministers' in Lello, J (ed) *Accountability in Education* London, Ward Lock Education.

Joseph, K (1982) '99th Conservative Party Address' *Education*, 8 October, p 265.

Kent County Council (1978) *Education Vouchers in Kent* Maidstone, Kent County Council.

Labour Party (1972) *Labour's Programme for Britain* London, The Labour Party.

Lawlor, S (1988) *Away With LEAs: ILEA Abolition as a Pilot* London, Centre for Policy Studies.

Meredith, P (1981) 'Executive discretion and choice of secondary school' *Public Law*, Spring, p 52.

Ministry of Education (1946) *Choice of Schools Circular 83* (14 January), London, HMSO.

Ministry of Education (1950) *Choice of Schools*, Manual of Guidance No. 1, London, HMSO.

Newell, P (1983) '1981 Act: no parents' charter on choice appeals' *Where?*, 185 (February).

The Observer (1993) Schools Report, 16 May, p 17.

Passmore, B (1983) 'Long hot summer of parental discontent' *Times Educational Supplement*, 19 August.

St John Stevas, N (1977) *Better Schools for All* London, Conservative Central Office.

Stillman A B and Maychell K (1986) *Choosing Schools: Parents, LEAs and the 1980 Education Act* Windsor, NFER–Nelson.

Sugarman, D (1979) 'How parental choice could enhance school power' *Education*, 153, (17–27 April), p 487.

Thomas, A and Dennison, W (1991) 'Parental or Pupil choice – who really decides in urban schools?' *Education Management and Administration*, 19, 4, pp 243–51.

Williams, S (1985) Interview with Jack Tweedie and Andy Stillman (unpublished).

Chapter 3

Parental Choice in the USA

Donald Biggs and Gerald Porter

At first glance, the topic of parental choice in schooling would appear to be quite foreign to American thinking, with its emphasis on education and the 'common school'. The history of education in the United States reveals a very early interest in the need for common schools to build a unifying sense of the public good. Schools have generally been seen as part of the process of creating model citizens who are hardworking, able to contribute to society, and most of all loyal to 'American Virtues'. Still, as Tyack (1988) points out, the history of public schooling in the United States cannot be explained simply as a form of political socialisation by the state. Throughout the nineteenth century citizens who thought their individual rights were being compromised voiced considerable resistance to compulsory education. Many nineteenth-century Americans endorsed strong beliefs in laissez-faire government and the inalienable rights of individuals to control their own private lives, including the education of their children.

In the early twentieth century, advocates of compulsory schooling in the United States assumed that all students in a pluralistic society needed similar educational experiences that would allow them to become responsible citizens with a sense of commitment to a common set of virtues. Parental choice through creating diversity in educational experiences was seen as a potential threat to the public good, and therefore school choice needed to be limited to schools that provided instruction in a common set of values and skills. The question for the 'family choice' advocates was whether families should have the right to choose the type of education that they wanted for their children. If so, parents then must be able to select schools which supported the values of their families. Advocates of this position saw their cause as an issue of individual rights. The historic dilemma for schools in the United States has been to balancé the value of providing common educational experiences that were necessary for establishing a common foundation of shared knowledge and values against the value of allowing choice for American parents to educate their children as they saw fit (see Levin, 1992).

Between 1850 and 1890 there was a remarkable sevenfold growth in school enrolment, and by the end of the century the typical child could be expected to attend school for at least five years. These changes in the level of attendance and the level of literacy occurred in the United States with little or no coercion by official bodies. Although 27 states had passed compulsory attendance legislation, many local officials seemed unaware of these laws. Indeed, historians describe how citizens of Massachusetts resisted complying with compulsory school attendance and how Barnstable, Massachusetts, was forced into compliance by the militia in the 1880s. Except in Connecticut and Massachusetts, the provisions for enforcement of compulsory school attendance were quite inadequate before 1890. Landes and Solomon (1972) concluded from their research that compulsory attendance laws probably did not positively influence the levels of school investment found in 1880 in the United States, but merely reflected changes in community attitudes about the values of common public education.

Family Choice in Education

Contemporary advocates of parental choice in schooling received increased visibility in the educational and political communities as a result of Coons and Sugarman's *Education by Choice* (1978). They argued that the public schools, because they aimed to socialise children in particular ways, were not neutral and did not foster the development of autonomy in future citizens. The issue of parental choice in schooling received national notice in June 1992 when President Bush proposed legislation entitled the 'Federal Grants for State and Local "GI Bills"' for children. It would have provided $1,000 federal scholarships to children of middle and low income families to be spent at public, private, or religious schools.

Levin (1991) gives three reasons why choice in education has become such an important contemporary political issue in the United States. First, there is the argument that, in a democracy, parents should have the right to choose the type of education that they want for their children. Parents should have the freedom to select schools that reinforce their traditions and values and need to be able to choose among schools that reflect the diversity of values in a pluralistic society. They should not be limited in their choices to the 'common' schools. Second, parents should be able to choose schools which best fit the educational needs of their children. Even among schools of a similar type, parents should have the opportunity to select a school of a particular size, curriculum, and/or pedagogical approach to match school experiences and their child's needs. Third, choice should lead to greater competition for students and thus to improvements in school achievement. Schools that are monopolies do not experience market pressures to improve their resources or the quality of their graduates.

The issues surrounding family choice and schooling are heatedly debated in the educational and political communities in the United States. However, the argument is not simply a matter of being for or against parental choice. Choice arrangements have been and are presently part of schooling in the United States. Should some of them be discontinued? Should some be supported more energetically? Should new choice arrangements be developed?

We will review school choice arrangements in the USA, indicating their similarities and differences in goals and expected outcomes as well as results of evaluation research. Raywid's (1985) excellent review of research is a major source of information used in this section.

During the first half of this century, tracking was one of the most obvious choice mechanisms in schools. The idea of tracking at the secondary level was to provide opportunities for students to enter appropriate programmes that were related to their post-high school plans. They could choose an academic, business/commercial, vocational, or general programme. The courts in the United States have challenged the practice of tracking on several legal grounds. Research has shown that minorities, the poor, and students of low ability often ended up with weaker teachers, found that less was expected of them, and found themselves directed towards less rewarding and lower-status jobs. For some, tracking appears to be a good choice mechanism because it allows students and families to choose their own education and if they do not do it well, or even if they restrict rather than widen their choices, that is the cost of individual freedom. Still, for others, tracking is inherently wrong because it is too closely tied to specific job or role preparation, it reflects pseudo-ability groupings, and generates an invidious status system.

Open Enrolment

One approach to family choice called Open Enrolment has been tried in such cities as Chicago, Kansas City, St Paul, New York, and Los Angeles. In 1960, New York City instigated an open enrolment plan that provided opportunities for parents of pupils in schools with a concentration of minority groups to transfer their children to schools with unused space that had more varied ethnic populations. In 1983, the New York City Free Choice Transfer Program was a model that tried to stabilise schools in changing neighbourhoods, maintain racially balanced enrolments, integrate schools, and equalise school use while maintaining ethnic balance. There was also a Reverse Open Enrolment plan that allowed white parents in predominantly white schools to select more integrated school settings for their children.

In the New York City Open Enrolment models, parents designated clusters of schools as their first, second, and third choices. The selection of schools in each cluster and the choice of a school within a cluster was made by the Board of Education's Office of Zoning and Integration. Sending schools had high percentages of minorities while receiving schools consisted of 70 per cent or more white students. Fox (1967) concluded that the New York City Open Enrolment plan did provide opportunities for better education. For instance, receiving schools at the junior high level were superior to sending schools with respect to teacher functioning, pupil functioning, and overall school quality. Still, the programme never attracted a substantial number of students. In the 1983–84 school year, about 1,143 students were part of the programme (Archer, 1983).

Magnet Schools

The 1976 amendment to the Federal Emergency School Aid Act

authorised grants to support the planning and implementation of magnet schools in districts involved in desegregation. Since that time, magnet schools have been used to draw students together in a variety of integrated settings. A study in 1982 identified more than 1,000 magnet schools in districts of 20,000 or more students (Fleming *et al*, 1982). They were more numerous in the Northeast, Midwest and West and most of them were at the elementary level where their major feature was a distinctive pedagogical style or environment. At the high school level, magnet schools tended to emphasise particular disciplines, career areas, or interdisciplinary themes.

The original emphasis on magnet schools was primarily on the goal of lessening segregation. However, over time the emphasis was expanded to include providing high quality educational alternatives. For example, magnets have been defined as those schools that offer special or distinctive programmes that are attractive to students of all races, that students may enter on a voluntary basis, and that serve to decrease segregation (McMillan, 1980).

Magnet schools have been found helpful in reducing the number of students in racially isolated schools and in aiding in district-wide desegregation efforts. They have been most successful in desegregating districts where the minority population numbers fewer than 30 per cent of the total student population and where there are several minorities (Fleming *et al*, 1982). Magnet school enrolments were found to average only 5 per cent of the total enrolments in the districts offering such programmes. Blank *et al* reported that interest in and commitment to magnet schools at the local level was higher than they anticipated. Magnets were seen by some local school boards as a viable approach to revitalisation and reform of schools. Staff, students and parents have been found to respond positively to magnet schools (Blank *et al*, 1983; see also Fleming *et al*, 1982).

Magnet schools have also been associated with some negative consequences or outcomes as well as the more positive ones. If magnet schools are too successful they may tend to become 'majority' or 'minority' ghettos. There have been cases where magnets actually contributed to an increase in the number of racially isolated schools, because a sizable portion of a relatively small group of minority students left regular schools and were then concentrated in the magnet schools, leaving the sending schools less integrated than they had been previously. In general, studies have found that the overall contribution of magnets to desegregation is slight (Raywid, 1985). Some might argue that the reason magnets are not effective educational mechanisms for desegregation is because of their voluntary choice provisions.

A Variety of School Alternatives

The alternatives movement in public schools began in the late 1960s. Parkway opened in Philadelphia in 1969 and Murray Road opened in Newton, Massachusetts in 1967. Alternative schools were to provide

- more personalised and humanistic settings;
- more exciting, satisfying, and challenging programmes;
- a better linkage between childhood and adult roles;
- a more accurate picture of the problems and injustices in the world;
- opportunities for students who had been unsuccessful in typical school programmes (Raywid, 1985).

For the most part, alternative schools were efforts at school reform rather than family choice mechanisms.

Schools within schools have tended to focus on either bright, interested students who wanted more from their education than conventional schools could offer or on providing special settings for underachieving drop-out prone and somewhat disruptive youngsters. The former used open admissions and were innovative, intellectually challenging and demanding educational environments. The latter were designed by administrators to solve specific problems of students rather than to improve the quality of their education. Admission to schools within schools was often limited to those who had been recommended by guidance counsellors or in some cases those students who had passed specific entrance examinations. The structure of a school within a school generally allows for considerable flexibility; they may emphasise varied themes, operate full or part time, focus on internships and work-study programmes, or focus on advanced placement courses.

One key element in the success of alternative schools seems to be the presence of enough professional autonomy that staff can create a distinctive educational environment. A school within a school is apt to have more difficulty than satellite alternatives or independent programmes in departing from normal school practices. The presence of common rules for decorum, similar scheduling practices, and similar disciplinary policies that are strictly enforced by building principals can become obstacles to the teachers who are trying to implement an innovative and effective school-within-a-school programme.

The YES (Your Educational Success) Programme was established in the 1990–91 school year at John Adams High School in South Bend, Indiana (Power and Power, 1992). Students qualify for the programme when they are unable to succeed in the normal high school because of low self-esteem, different learning styles, lack of motivation, or lack of confidence. Three special teachers offer individualised and small-group instruction to 27 students, a third of whom are African-American, Hispanic, and Asian. Fewer than 15 per cent of these students live with both parents and about 40 per cent have been in trouble with the law.

Mini-schools were developed as a means for increasing personalisation and participation of students in their educational environments by dividing schools into small units (Raywid, 1985). Haaren High School in New York was divided into 14 mini-schools such as college-bound, aviation, automotive, work-study, traditional, and urban affairs. Mini-schools may emphasise curricular differences or differences in instructional settings and approaches. Mini-schools at the elementary level have usually differed in their instructional approaches rather than their curricular offerings.

Different school site alternatives have been either satellites or actual separate schools. The first contemporary public choice systems were an outcome of the 1971 United States Office of Education Experimental Schools programme. In Minneapolis, all elementary schools were eventually placed on an options basis because of the success of a pilot programme in one area of the city. Their goals were to provide family choice, decentralise school governance, increase parent participation, improve educational quality, and desegregate schools. The Minneapolis Southeast Alternatives Project included staff and parent participation; parent, teacher, and student choice was an important element in the planning and implementation process (Raywid, 1985).

Satellite schools have usually been annexes with administrative ties to parent schools. The director reports to the school principal and resources of the parent school may be available to students and staff housed in satellite units. In some cases these separate or autonomous alternative schools may find themselves outside the bureaucratic structures that allocate resources.

A number of school choice programmes have involved inter-district arrangements. Several school districts may sponsor a single alternative school. Districts may allow out-of-district students to enrol in their schools on a fee-paying basis. In several states, including Connecticut, Massachusetts, and Wisconsin, cross-district enrolments have been allowed as a means of promoting desegregation. Wisconsin has provided financial incentives to both sending and receiving districts. When a student transfer between districts contributes to desegregation, the sending district continues to receive state aid while the receiving district is also reimbursed by the state for the full cost of educating and transporting the student (Bennett, 1984).

In Herkimer County located in Central New York State, 12 public school districts offer a choice of enrolment without fees to non-residents, with the goal of improving citizen satisfaction with their schools. Parents may choose to have their children attend the designated schools in their home districts or they may send them to schools in one of the 11 other districts. Acceptance is based solely on available space without regard to students' past academic or behavioural records.

Over 13,000 students attend schools in these 12 districts, and in 1992–93 about 344 students (2.7 per cent) from 219 families chose to attend schools in districts outside their residence. Davis (1993), in an evaluation of the Herkimer County inter-district arrangements, found that families who chose to enrol their children in schools outside their home districts were typically more wealthy, had more education, had higher incomes, and were more involved in the education of their children. Parents appeared to use similar criteria when deciding either to keep their children in their home districts or to transfer them to other districts. The quality of academic programmes, teacher quality, the conditions in the schools, and proximity of schools to home or work sites of parents were most influential in both these school choices.

Many parents seek schooling for their children on the basis of religious rather than purely educational criteria. Although concerned about educational quality, these parents are more concerned that school practices and curriculum do not undermine their religious teachings and values. So far, most parents who send their children to private religious schools have received little if any support from either state or local government. However, in 1983, the US Supreme Court upheld a Minnesota law permitting tax deductions for private religious schools (Bernstein, 1992).

Many parents with children attending sectarian schools have wanted 'tuition vouchers' to offset costs. In March 1991, the Wisconsin legislature established a school choice programme on a limited basis for economically disadvantaged students in the Milwaukee school district. The programme provided vouchers to the district equal to the state's cost per pupil of $2,500 (Staff, 1991). The plan was no help to families with children in religious schools since only private, non-sectarian schools were eligible to participate. To enable Catholic schools in Milwaukee to be included, the Archdiocese endorsed a strategy to convert local diocesan schools to non-sectarian entities (Bernstein, 1992).

Many experts, such as David Boaz of the Cato Institute and Clint Bolick, Vice President of the Institute for Justice, believe that the courts will ultimately sanction vouchers for religious schools. However, some parents of children in these schools may wonder if publicly funded vouchers will lead to government control over these schools (Staff, 1991).

Educational Vouchers

Proponents of vouchers have argued that a competitive market approach to schooling will improve overall quality of the graduates. Under a voucher system, parents will have more choice over the education that their children receive than they do at present.

In 1990, the voucher issue received a great deal of attention in the educational community with the publication of *Politics, Markets and America's Schools* by John Chubb and Terry Moe. They argued that democratic control had been an obstacle to improving schools in the United States. Democracy had allowed schools to become subject to endless demands from the populace and this had led to the creation of a large, unresponsive, inefficient, school-based organisation.

Chubb and Moe proposed a model of public choice that would be characterised by the free movement of students and resources throughout any public school in a state. Transportation would be provided and family decisions facilitated through a state infrastructure featuring 'Choice Offices' and 'Parent Information Centers'. Parent liaisons would meet families to assist in making evaluations of the assets and liabilities of different schools and to help coordinate application procedures for different schools. Schools would develop their own mission statements, set their own fees, and make their own admissions decisions subject to nondiscrimination requirements. Their application process would need to allow students a fair shot at getting the school of their choice. Student scholarships would include federal, state, and local funds and would be allocated directly to the parents' school choice.

Educational vouchers have been described as a market-based approach to school choice because this plan is governed by competitive forces. Vouchers, as described by Friedman (1955; 1962, Ch 6), provide families with certificates that can be used to pay tuition at any school that meets minimal requirements. One hoped-for outcome would be that schools would compete to attract and retain students and parents would be able to achieve better schooling for their children. The state would provide the funds for educational vouchers, establish criteria for eligibility of schools, provide information on schools to parents, adjudicate in conflicts between parents and schools, and monitor attendance.

Voucher plans differ along three dimensions: finance, regulation and information (Levin, 1991). The financial aspects of vouchers differ in terms of size or amounts, intended uses, and whether vouchers will cover complete or partial costs. In some plans, parents would receive a uniform voucher and they could provide 'add-ons'; in other plans, children of poor families would receive larger amounts. Voucher plans differ as regards their criteria for identifying eligible schools. Finally, voucher plans differ in their approaches to providing information needed for parents and schools to make effective choices. The challenge in a voucher system is to provide succinct, clear and accurate information to a wide variety of parents and students about changing educational environments in different schools. In order to create an effective voucher system, parents need adequate information, and in some cases they also need special assistance from counsellors in the interpretation of this information.

In order to evaluate educational voucher plans, it is necessary to address the specific attributes of plans such as their financing arrangements, types of regulations and the means used for providing information about educational options. Advocates of educational vouchers argue that a market approach to schooling will particularly benefit children from poor families who are victims of poor schools and lack meaningful school choices. In spite of these lofty goals, one conclusion that can be drawn from the limited research on the topic is that even in the most favourable cases, school choice mechanisms such as vouchers probably do not come close to equalising educational opportunities across income groups. It appears from the results of empirical studies that the poor are least likely to pursue educational options (see Levin, 1992).

A Private Voucher Model

The Educational CHOICE Charitable Trust of Indianapolis, Indiana, is the first privately funded voucher programme in the United States. Initiated in 1991, the goal of CHOICE Charitable Trust is to enable low-income parents to place their children in private schools. The chairman of the Golden Rule Insurance Company argues that, 'When all families, no matter how poor, have the freedom to walk away from bad schools, competition will force the public schools to improve' (Kaelble, 1991, p 12).

In order to qualify, families must reside within the Indianapolis Public Schools district, have children who are entering grades K to 8, and be eligible for free or reduced-cost lunches under the federal income guidelines. Once eligible, the Trust will pay half the cost of private-school tuition up to a maximum of $800 per year per child. The grants are awarded without academic or other requirements. If too many students apply, the grants will be allocated on a lottery basis. Not more than 50 per cent of the grants are permitted for students already enrolled in private schools. The remaining 50 per cent will go to new students (Golden Rule Insurance Company, 1991). At its initial level of funding the Golden Rule programme provided vouchers for 500 low-income families. Subsequent donations from other Indiana businesses have increased the eligible pool (as of the 1991–92 school year) to about 800 students. The apparent success of the Educational CHOICE Trust has inspired similar programmes in other American cities such as Albany, New York; Atlanta, Georgia; Little Rock, Arkansas; Milwaukee, Wisconsin; and San Antonio, Texas (Lamb, 1993).

Home Education

Perhaps the ultimate choice option for parents is the removal of their children altogether from institutional schooling. Education at home has always been an option, but the perception of the legitimacy of this option has changed dramatically over the last 200 years as the pre-eminence of public or state-sponsored education has been established.

Before the 1820s, formal education for Americans was a viable option only for the rich, and it usually occurred in the classroom of a private school or by instruction at home. With the establishment of compulsory education in the late nineteenth century, it was still possible for well-to-do families to educate their children at home. Many prominent Americans, including presidents and military heroes, have been educated at home (Texas Home School Coalition, 1986). In New York State, only with the passage of compulsory education laws did the status of home education become more uncertain. But clearly, in the post-Second World War period, there was a renewed optimism in the efficacy of government and public institutions to serve individual needs, and the habit of teaching children at home virtually died out in *all* sectors of society.

But by the late 1960s and early 1970s public optimism about common schools had faded, with an increasing perception of the negative effects of schooling. This was a major shift from previous critiques of education which focused on issues such as quality of education and access to educational services. With the deschooling movement articulated by theorists like Ivan Illich came a critique of education that held that more was not better and charged that the process of institutional schooling itself was flawed and could be destructive to the proper development of children. This trend led initially to the development of non-traditional schools, the so-called 'free school' movement, that all but died from undercapitalisation and a lack of synchrony with mainstream values emphasising schooling as preparation for the workplace rather than for personal development.

But many parents were totally disillusioned with all attempts at formal schooling, accepting the humanistic, deschooling critique but having nowhere to turn but to themselves. Still other families rejected the humanistic critique and also rejected public schools which they perceived as immoral and undisciplined. These two diverse and sometimes contradictory groups make up the bulk of home educators today. They may be roughly characterised as the independents and the fundamentalists. The independents are largely ideological descendants of the protesters of the 1960s who tend to see schools as undesirable options because they are authoritarian, dehumanising, and over-regimented. The fundamentalists are usually more concerned with protecting their children from the perceived moral decline of the larger society that is manifested in public schools as lax discipline, low behavioural expectations, and low academic standards.

However, the fundamentalists and the independents share several major concerns. Both seek to resist the trend that Berger and Berger (1983) have described as the tendency for modern institutions such as state schools to increasingly assume functions for which the family has traditionally been responsible. Both independents and fundamentalists share the 'objective of developing or maintaining close relationships within the family' and agree that a 'child's education should be the responsibility of the parents not the school' (Mayberry and Knowles, 1989, p 217). A common goal of home educators is the objective of building or deepening family bonds. The experiences occurring within the context of the family are seen as more important than the purely instrumental concerns of curriculum content or instructional methodology.

At least 50,000 children in the USA are home schooled (Lines, 1987), but most experts agree this figure is probably a drastic underestimate. There is no reliable reporting mechanism and many home educators are wary of bureaucratic entanglements and refuse to report to authorities.

Perhaps the most impressive empirical support for home schooling was reported by Gene Frost (1988), who examined 74 home-schooled children from 58 families. Frost evaluated the students with the Iowa Test of Basic Skills and found the home schoolers above expectancy at all four grades examined. Home schoolers in grade 3 on average performed at the 4.5 grade level or at the 74th percentile. Sixth graders obtained an average grade equivalency of 7.6 at the 70th percentile, and comparable results were found for grades 4 and 5. Linden (1983), as reported in Ray (1988), administered the California Achievement Test to 16 home-educated youths in grades 1.9 to 11.6 and obtained scores in reading, mathematics, and language that were on average a full grade above the norm. Ray (1988) reported an evaluation study of the Parent as Tutor Program conducted by the Washington State Superintendent of Public Education. Using results from the Stanford Achievement Tests for grades K to 8, the home-educated pupils obtained consistently above-average percentile scores (reading 62, language 56.5, and mathematics 53).

We would like to conclude this chapter with a few brief personal observations regarding parental choice and education in the USA. Traditionally in the United States, parents have had both the right and responsibility to educate their children as they thought best. Parents as citizens turned to government, not for directions but for help in meeting their common need to educate future generations. The management of public education in the USA has traditionally been a bottom-up affair through local school boards. But public education has increasingly become the stepchild of state and national bureaucrats and technocrats who presume to 'know better' than parents by virtue of their professional expertise. The state and its representatives have claimed the right to control and prescribe the educative process, allegedly on the basis of the common good usually defined in economic terms.

References

Archer, F (1983) *Breakdown in assignments in the Free Choice Program for 1983-1984* (memorandum, October 17) New York, New York City Schools.

Bennett, D A (1984) 'A plan for increasing educational opportunities and improving racial balance in Milwaukee' in Willie, C A (ed) *School Desegregation Plans that Work* Westport, CT, Greenwood.

Berger, B and Berger, P (1983) *The War over the Family* New York, Doubleday.

Bernstein, D (1992) 'Religion in school: a role for vouchers' *Current* 4, 342, p 13.

Blank, R, Dentler, R A, Baltzell, O C, and Chabobar, K (1983) *Survey of Magnet Schools – Final Report: Analyzing a Model for Quality Integrated Education* Washington, DC, James H. Lowry and Associates.

Chubb, J and Moe, T (1990) *Politics, Markets and America's Schools* Washington, DC, The Brookings Institution.

Coons, J E and Sugarman, S D (1978) *Education by Choice* Berkeley, CA, University of California Press.

Davis, G H (1993) *Patterns of Non-resident School Attendance in Central New York as a Model of Open Enrollment* Doctoral dissertation, University at Albany, Albany, NY.

Fleming, P, Blank, R, Dentler, R A and Baltzell, O (1982) *Survey of Magnet Schools: Interim Report* (September) Washington, DC, James H. Lowry and Associates.

Fox, D J (1967) *Expansion of the Free Choice Open Enrollment Program* New York, Center for Urban Education.

Friedman, M (1955) 'The role of government in education' in Soto, R A (ed) *Economics and the Public Interest* New Brunswick, NJ, Rutgers University Press.

Friedman, M (1962) *Capitalism and Freedom* Chicago, University of Chicago Press.

Frost, G (1988) 'Academic success of students in home schooling' *Illinois School Research and Development*, 24, 3, pp 111–17.

Golden Rule Insurance Company (1991) *$1.2 Million Pledge from Insurance Company gives Inner-city Children Access to Private Education* (press release).

Kaelble, S (1991) 'Enough talk' *Indiana Business Magazine*, pp 10–47.

Lamb, G (1993) 'Privately funded educational choice programs: a conference report' *The Threefold Review*, pp 44–46.

Landes, W, and Solomon, L (1972) 'Compulsory schooling legislation: an economic analysis of law and social change in the nineteenth century' *Journal of Economic History*, 32, pp 58–88.

Levin, H M (1991) 'The economics of educational choice' *Economics of Education Review*, 10, 2, pp 137–158.

Levin, H M (1992) 'Market approaches to education: vouchers and school choice' *Economics of Education Review*, 11, 4, 279–85.

Lines, P M (1987) 'An overview of home instruction' *Phi Delta Kappa*, 68, pp 510–517.

Mayberry, M, and Knowles, J (1989) 'Family unity objectives of parents who teach their children: ideological and pedagogical orientations to home schooling' *Urban Review*, 21, 4, pp 209–25.

McMillan, C B (1980) *Magnet Schools: An Approach to Voluntary Desegregation* Bloomington, Phi Delta Kappa.

Power, F C and Power, A M R (1992) 'A raft of hope: democratic education and the challenge of pluralism' *Journal of Moral Education*, 21, 3, pp 193–205.

Ray, B D (1988) 'Home schools: a synthesis of research on characteristics and learner outcomes' *Education and Urban Society*, 21, 1, pp 16–31.

Raywid, M A (1985) 'Family choice arrangements in public schools: a review of the literature' *Review of Educational Research*, 55, pp 435–67.

Staff (1991) 'State and local plans' *CO Researcher*, 10 May, pp 263–66.

Texas Home School Coalition (1986) *Home Education: Is it Working?* Richardson, TX, THSC.

Tyack, D B (1988) 'Ways of seeing: an essay on the history of compulsory schooling' in Jaeger, R M (ed) *Complementary Methods for Research in Education* Washington, DC, American Educational Research Association.

Chapter 4

Education and the Ideology of Parentocracy

Phillip Brown

In this chapter it will be argued that we are entering a 'third wave' in the socio-historical development of British education and that similar trends are also evident in the United States, Eastern Europe and the Antipodes. The 'first wave' can be characterised by the rise of mass schooling for the working classes in the late nineteenth century. The 'second wave' involved a shift from the provision of education based upon what Dewey (1916) called the 'feudal dogma of social predestination' to one organised on the basis of individual merit and achievement. What is distinct about the 'third wave' is the move towards a system whereby the education a child receives must conform to the *wealth* and *wishes* of parents rather than the *abilities* and *efforts* of pupils. In other words, we have witnessed a shift away from the 'ideology of meritocracy' to what I will call the 'ideology of parentocracy'. This has involved a major programme of educational 'privatisation' under the slogans of 'choice', 'freedom', 'standards', and 'excellence'.

The defining feature of the ideology of parentocracy and the market policies it seeks to legitimate is not the amount of education received, but the social basis upon which educational selection is organised. An expansion of higher education, for instance, is already beginning to take place. Although this is likely to lead to a larger proportion of middle and working class students entering higher education (assuming that the latter are willing and able to pay off substantial financial debts at the end of their studies), it does not represent an equality of opportunity. It simply means that differences between institutions of higher education will increase rather like those found in the United States (Brown *et al*, 1994). It is also important to note that the ideology of parentocracy has not emerged as a result of a groundswell of popular demand for radical educational reform among a majority of parents, and does not imply an increase in parent power over the school curriculum or 'choice' of school. On the contrary, it is not parents but the state that has strengthened its control over what is taught in schools, and it will be schools who choose pupils, rather than parents which choose schools, when it comes to gaining access to more popular educational establishments.

In this chapter these three 'waves' of educational ideology and policy will be briefly outlined in order to provide a general picture of educational change in England. As a contribution to subsequent debates this chapter will also address the question of why the ideology of parentocracy has informed policy debates in the late twentieth century, and consider what implication it may have for our understanding of the relationship between education, the family and the state.

The First Wave

The 'first wave' is characterised by the development of mass schooling in the nineteenth century. This was intended to confirm rather than transcend existing social divisions (Hurt, 1981). The education a child received had to conform to his or her predetermined place in the social order. Elementary education was thus largely defined in terms of instruction to meet the minimum requirements perceived to be necessary in order for the labouring poor to fulfil their future roles in a changing society. The school was seen as a device to reform manners, promote religion and ensure discipline (Johnson, 1976). Secondary education, which remained a preserve of the middle classes until well into the twentieth century, existed primarily to provide an education perceived to be suitable for a 'gentleman' and for entry into the professions, and thus to ensure the reproduction of social and economic elites.

If social class was the dominant organising principle during the 'first wave', it was cross-cut in a vitally important way by gender. The education of the male was seen to be of primary importance given the patriarchal structure of the family, and there was a commonly held assumption at the time that women were biologically inferior to men both in physique and intellect (Purvis, 1983). Deem (1978), among others, has noted the importance of the 'domestic ideology' for shaping the form and content of education for girls, which identified a woman's role with the domestic sphere regardless of social class. Purvis (1983) distinguishes the liberal education provided for middle-class women, who needed to learn the complex rituals of etiquette, the management of the household and of domestic servants and the participation in 'good works' in the locality, from the basic instruction in practical domestic skills provided for working class women. Schooling during the 'first wave' was thus structured on the basis of ascription for one's predetermined future social, occupational and domestic roles.

The Second Wave

The 'second wave' involved an ideological shift in organising principle, from an education determined by an accident of birth (ascription) to one based upon one's age, aptitude and ability (achievement). In a 'meritocratic' system of education (Young, 1961), all must be given an equal opportunity of gaining access to jobs concomitant with their abilities. However, the meritocracy never promised equality, only that inequalities would be distributed more fairly.

The importance attached to individual achievement as a determinant of one's educational and occupational career was particularly evident in the writings of Parsons (1961) and informed much of the debate about education in the post-war period 1944–76 (Bernbaum, 1977). Parsons argued that in an advanced industrial society the school confronted a dual problem of selecting the most able individuals and facilitating their educational and social advancement, as well as the problem of internalising the commitment and capacities necessary for the successful performance of their future adult roles.

The shift from a system of 'sponsored' mobility towards a system of 'contest' mobility in Britain (Turner, 1961, p 122), which necessitated a system of comprehensive education, was not ultimately achieved on an appeal to social justice or the acquisition of a common culture (cf Tawney, 1931, p 145), but on the grounds that educational expansion was necessary in order to ensure Britain's economic prosperity. This argument was based on the assumption that the general level of skill and knowledge required for most occupations would increase as the number of unskilled jobs declined rapidly. It was also assumed that an investment in education was both a sure way of maintaining economic competitiveness and, for the individual, an insurance policy against unemployment. A logical outcome of the economic argument for educational expansion was the development of educational policies aimed at ending the restrictive practices which prevented able working class pupils from realising their educational and economic potential. Such policies were needed because sociological evidence showed that the tripartite system established by the 1944 Education Act was neither freeing working class talent nor generating equality of opportunity (Halsey *et al*, 1961). This could only be achieved in conditions of an open contest, which required a shift to comprehensive education.

The expansion of comprehensive education in the 1960s and 1970s has led to a general improvement in educational standards, although the working classes have not significantly improved their relative educational or life chances. Also, during the 'second wave', gender inequalities have declined, despite the fact that important gender divisions remain (Arnot and Weiner, 1987). Gender divisions in the organisation and process of schooling have become less explicit, more open to question, and subject to policy reform.

The Third Wave

The 'third wave' has involved a shift in organising principle, from the ideology of meritocracy to the ideology of parentocracy, where a child's education is increasingly dependent upon the wealth and wishes of parents, rather than the ability and efforts of pupils. Therefore, in the centuries-old battleground between the principle of selection by family and the principle of selection by merit (Young, 1961), the former is once more in the ascendancy. If the dual objectives of 'equality of opportunity' and 'economic efficiency' were the two-edged sword thrust at the heart of elite educational sponsorship in the 1960s, it has been turned against the advocates of comprehensive education, because on both counts the educational system has failed to live up to its promise. The massive investment in education during the 1960s did not prevent the economic recession signalled by the oil crisis of 1973 and the subsequent increase in youth unemployment, which in the early 1980s amounted to the virtual collapse of the youth labour market in many parts of Britain. By the mid-1970s the educational consensus was dead, and James Callaghan's Great Debate on Education which was launched in 1976 signalled 'noise of crisis' (Donald, 1981), which was yet to be fully articulated or understood. There were a growing number of complaints from employers which blamed the schools for failing to meet the needs of industry (Hopkins, 1978). The ascendancy of the political right also gave credence to the idea that the attempts to 'tap the pool of ability' believed to exist among the working class in the 1960s were now a source of economic liability (Brown, 1987; Finn, 1987).

Equally, the proponents of comprehensive education could find little comfort from the research evidence concerning the extent to which the 'meritocracy' had become a reality, and little support from the academic community which by the time of the Great Debate was coming to grips with what Marxists were telling them about the role of education in a capitalist society. The Marxist message was that the 'meritocracy' was largely symbolic, given the structural correspondence which was assumed to exist between education and production (Bowles and Gintis, 1976).

The radical right's account of the educational crisis (see Cox and Dyson, 1968; Cox and Boyson, 1977) has asserted that the comprehensive 'experiment' had not only failed, but was the cause of a decline in educational standards:

> It must always be remembered that the deterioration in British education has arisen partly because schools have been treated as instruments for equalising, rather than instructing, children. Merit, competition and self-esteem have been devalued or repudiated; the teaching of facts has given way to the inculcation of opinion; education has often been confounded with indoctrination; and in many places there is a serious risk of disciplined study being entirely swamped by an amorphous tide of easy-going discussion and idle play. (The Hillgate Group, 1987, p 2)

The right have also attempted to impute a socialist revolutionary character to the shift towards comprehensive education (Flew, 1987, p 27), though this interpretation sits uneasily with the participation of post-war Conservative governments in its establishment.

Such difficulties do not affect their contention that the comprehensive experiment has failed. Indeed, because of the hopelessly optimistic belief that comprehensive education could overcome broader social inequalities and Britain's economic troubles, the proponents of liberal democratic reforms have found it difficult to counter the right's critique. The right have argued that the comprehensive experiment has not only failed the working classes, but betrayed them by giving them an education which is not suited to their 'needs'. This has also led to an erosion of the standards of our elite schools because of their 'contamination' by the masses (see Bantock, 1977).

The issue of declining educational standards has been at the heart of the right's attack on comprehensive education for many years (Cox and Dyson, 1968; Jones, 1989), in spite of the lack of credible evidence to support the assertion that educational standards have declined (see Wright, 1983, p 175), let alone to show that any decline is the result of comprehensive reorganisation. This is because 'standards' are as much a moral issue as an educational one. The main concern of the authoritarian right is to regain traditional authority, leadership and the reproduction of elite culture, in which the educational system is seen to have a key role to play. For them, it is the very idea of comprehensive education which violates their notion of standards, not only its imputed consequences (Brown, 1989). It is the shift from elite to mass culture, and the erosion of respect for authority which they oppose. This desire often contradicts the goals of the 'free marketeers' whose ideas derive from classical liberalism (see Scruton, 1984; Belsey, 1986; Green, 1987). Here emphasis is placed on free enterprise, individual choice and self-interest. According to the principles of classical liberalism, the state should limit its involvement to ensuring that families have equal access to the market for education and training, because the market is always assumed to lead to outcomes superior to those achieved through government planning. This, it is asserted, will improve the efficiency of schools because it will avoid 'provider capture' where public sector institutions are organised by state professionals in their own interests rather than the interest of the consumer (ie parents and students), and lead to an increase in educational standards because parents will demonstrate a greater interest in their child's education (see Lauder, 1991; Brown and Lauder, 1992).

An uneasy alliance between the authoritarian conservatives and the 'market' men and women has been possible due to their mutual disdain of 'collective social reform'. Classical liberals oppose such reforms because they 'consider them to be menaces to freedom, conservatives, because they consider them to be egalitarian in tendency' (Phillips, 1978, p 12). The potential conflict among the right has so far been limited because despite their ideological differences both serve the political and material interests of the powerful and privileged (Gamble, 1988). In a 'free market' society, although we may have formal equality before the law, we do not have substantive equality. Moreover, the privatisation of education has an appeal to the authoritarian conservatives, because the latter believe that if left to the free market, not only would the traditional schools be preserved, but also the schooling for different social groups would 'diversify as society required' (Scruton, 1984, p 160).

Those who advocate the ideology of parentocracy seek to establish what they describe as an 'independent education for all' (Hillgate Group, 1987, p 2). This would mean that the Local Education Authorities (LEAs) would no longer be the main providers of 'education' and the comprehensive system would be scrapped. In order to establish an 'independent education for all' it is necessary to think of schools as separate educational firms, subject like the presently existing private schools to the incentives and discipline of the market. It is argued that a major advantage of this kind of educational arrangement is that it maximises variety and choice while rejecting all attempts to impose and sustain what its proponents see as a state 'monopoly' and a 'uniform service' for all its consumers. Hence two conditions need to exist in order to achieve an 'independent education for all'. First, all parents should be free and able to move their children from one school to another if they so desire, and second, every school should have strong financial incentives to attract and to hold custom, and have sufficient reason to fear disaster if it fails (Flew, 1987, p 7). It is assumed that open competition between schools will raise standards for all and offer real choices to parents. However, those schools which fail to recruit enough pupils should be allowed to go out of business.

An 'independent education for all' has yet to be introduced, although many of the ideas which inform it are currently shaping the future direction of education in Britain – and in other countries (see Shor, 1986; Botstein, 1988; Lauder *et al*, 1988). The 1988 Educational Reform Act in England and Wales laid the foundations for the local management of schools which has removed many of the powers of the LEAs; introduced 'open enrolment' to allow popular schools to recruit more students irrespective of the fact that a decline in student numbers in other local schools may make them 'uneconomic' and subject to closure; and offered financial incentives for schools to 'opt out' of the control of the LEA and to become 'independent' (ie a grant maintained school). The attempt to accelerate the numbers of primary as well as secondary schools seeking independent status was signalled in 1992. A further element of recent Education Acts has been the introduction of formal testing and assessment of pupils at the ages of 7, 11, 14, and 16. This represents part of the attempt to provide parents with the consumer information necessary for an informed choice of school for their child.

All the above represent steps towards the creation of an education market (Pring, 1987; Ball, 1993). Simon has noted that the main thrust of the 1988 Education Reform Act was towards 'destabilising locally controlled "systems" and, concomitantly, pushing the whole structure of schooling towards a degree, at least, of privatisation, so establishing a base which could be further exploited later' (1988, p 48). What Simon is hinting at here is the possibility of moving towards the introduction of educational vouchers. The 'opting out' proposal as envisaged by Margaret Thatcher is not quite a voucher system but it is similar to it (Wilby and Midgley, 1987). The kind of educational voucher system which is being advocated by the right is one which approximates to that favoured by Friedman – a straightforward scheme which gives every child the same 'pupil entitlement' (The Hillgate Group, 1987, p 41). Simon has also noted that while the right want a *variety* of schools they also demand a 'strict *uniformity* in the curriculum' (1988, p 17). Therefore, despite the rhetoric of 'choice' and 'individual freedom', in practice the educational system is becoming *more* centrally controlled, and both teachers and parents will have less control over the school curriculum.

The Ideology of Parentocracy: The Sociological Context

It is important to note that there is nothing inevitable about the direction of educational change (Simon, 1985). Indeed, there are genuine possibilities that education in the 'third wave' will be based on an alternative politics of education to that currently directing policy because of the inherent contradictions within a market system of education. The social and economic transformation of Western industrial societies which we are currently experiencing will make the need for an alternative to the ideology of parentocracy all the more urgent. It has been argued elsewhere that there are new historical possibilities for the emergence of a more democratic, efficient and equitable system of formal education (Brown and Lauder, 1992).

Moreover, when policies are applied in practice, intentions and outcomes are rarely the same, as anyone who has studied the recent history of educational reforms will testify (Shilling, 1989). Policy implementation often results in unintended consequences which may be difficult to predict, and which may mitigate the worst excesses of market policies (Whitty, 1989). Such policies are also likely to meet with considerable resistance from working class parents and children, who have most to lose from these reforms. Indeed, when the realities of 'parental choice' become clearer, the demand for real choices and opportunities for their children are likely to increase (David, 1980). With these caveats in mind, I want to tentatively consider two questions: first, why has the ideology of parentocracy come to dominate the educational agenda during the late twentieth century? and second, what are its implications for educational selection and legitimation?

To answer the question of why we are abandoning comprehensive education will require a broader framework than that outlined above. In particular there appear to be at least three points which need elaboration. First, the ideology of parentocracy and the introduction of market policies have developed against a background of high youth unemployment and economic recession. In this respect they have been a response to traditional concerns about the social consequences of youth unemployment, particularly in urban areas, and the failure of the school to meet the needs of industry (Dale, 1985). Such political concerns are not unique to Britain. The enhanced role of technical and vocational education in secondary education has been almost universal (Lauglo and Lillis, 1988). However, in Britain the relationship between education and industry has been incorporated into a larger political debate about the relative merits of selective versus comprehensive education, and a state monopoly of education versus a privatised education system. Those opposed to post-war reforms in education have not been slow to exploit the disquiet expressed about the products of education, in order to support a powerful (and largely successful) lobby which has undermined the ideological foundations of the second wave. A major concern of the right has been to ensure a much clearer relationship between educational and social hierarchy and authority, which is why they have demanded more selection and greater 'diversity'. However, the explicit attempt to reorganise the educational system on the basis of social ascription is politically unacceptable, which is why they have opted for *social selection by stealth*, through market solutions. Beneath the rhetoric of 'parental choice', 'academic excellence' and 'individual freedom' is the belief that opening up the educational system to the discipline of the market will solve the problem of social authority and hierarchy; that different types of schools would emerge for different types of people. Flew has candidly admitted that the break-up of the comprehensive system in favour of different types of specialist schools is what 'the radical right in education has been begging for years, and which would very soon emerge if once the existing individual state schools had to compete for custom' (1987, p 22).

Yet to seek to explain the introduction of market reform solely in terms of political ideology is inadequate. My second point is that the abandonment of the ideology of meritocracy has been inextricably connected to the question of 'statecraft' which Bulpitt has defined as 'the art of winning elections and, above all, achieving a necessary degree of governing competence in office' (1986, p 19; see also Harris, 1989).

There is little doubt that in the context of rising unemployment, economic decline and the escalation in educational expenditure, a commitment to extending 'equality of educational opportunities' was difficult to maintain. Comprehensive education had become a political liability to Callaghan's Labour government, especially because, unlike a number of other countries such as Sweden (Ball and Larsson, 1989), the principle of comprehensive education had never gained unquestioning political or public support. The working classes did not embrace the comprehensive school as the road to their liberation, and the left held out little hope that the educational system would or could significantly improve the life-chances of working class people (Bowles and Gintis, 1976; Bourdieu and Passeron, 1977).

By the time Mrs Thatcher became Prime Minister in 1979 there was little political mileage to be gained by the attempt to bolster the post-war educational consensus: education had become a scapegoat for Britain's social and economic problems, and thus was an area of social policy about which something had to be done. Therefore purely in terms of Conservative statecraft, a governing competence over education was facilitated by identifying post-war liberal democratic reforms as the cause of current troubles, which provided an argument for radical educational change.

My third point is based on a more general observation of the relationship between education, certification and social change. The 'third wave' is in part a manifestation of a power struggle for educational certification which is undermining the principles of 'equality of educational opportunity'. Whereas the social elite have continued to enjoy the benefits of private education throughout the twentieth century, the demand to equip their incumbents with academic credentials has increased (Walford, 1986). The changing demand for academic credentials among the middle class as a whole has been noted by Bourdieu and Boltanski (1978) who argue that the increasing demand for education is closely linked to broader changes in social structure, namely the bureaucratisation and rationalisation of the recruitment practices used by large corporations and professional organisations. The acquisition of educational credentials has become an important insurance policy, minimising the likelihood of unemployment.

An equally important change has resulted from the restructuring of occupations and economic life (Sabel, 1982; Piore and Sabel, 1984; Gallie, 1988; Pahl, 1988). One outcome has been to undermine traditional patterns of career progression within public and private sector organisations. As corporations are subject to 'take-over', 'break-up' or 'restructuring', the consequences for employees are frequently enforced 'career moves', 'redundancy', or 'early retirement'. The acquisition of externally validated qualifications is being increasingly used as a way of insulating managers and company executives against the vagaries of the global market and corporate restructuring (Brown *et al*, 1994). This trend not only helps us to explain the increasing demand for business studies at both undergraduate and postgraduate levels, but also the increasingly instrumental attitudes of middle class parents concerning the education of their children.

The onslaught against comprehensive education by the popular press, coupled with the teachers' industrial action in the mid-1980s, added to the anxieties of many middle class parents, which resulted in an increasing propensity to send their children to private (independent) schools, especially between the ages of 16 and 18. In England almost 20 per cent of pupils between these ages were already in private education in 1986.

In a political climate where we have been told that there is 'no such thing as society, only families and individuals' (see Harris, 1989), those parents who can afford to buy a competitive advantage for their children are increasingly likely to do so, because the right have claimed a moral legitimacy for a privatised education system under the rhetorical slogans of 'parental choice', 'standards of excellence' and 'economic freedom'. The bare facts, however, are that a growing section of the 'old' and 'new' middle classes are undermining the principle of 'equality of opportunity', in the sense that educational outcomes should be determined by the abilities and efforts of pupils, not the wealth and preferences of parents. This form of 'social closure' is the outcome of an evaluation by the middle classes that educational success has become too important to be left to the chance outcome of a formally open competition (despite what the research evidence has taught us about social class and patterns of achievement). The fact that potentially more able students who do not have the same financial means will lose out just becomes another hard fact of life, because it is not the responsibility of the state to regulate the competition for education in a fair and equal manner, but to ensure the sovereignty of 'parental choice'. It is this change in the relationship between education and the state which we now want to consider.

Education and the State: Control without responsibility

Market reforms in education clearly have important implications for the way sociologists have interpreted the role of education in advanced capitalist societies, and more specifically the relationship between education and the state (Dale, 1989). Liberal accounts have emphasised the importance of state control of education in order to ensure its organisation on meritocratic principles. This form of state involvement has been taken for granted because it is assumed that if society is to function efficiently it is essential to get the best people in the most demanding jobs, irrespective of class, gender or racial attributes. Marxist accounts have alternatively emphasised the role of the state in securing the reproduction of social inequalities by legitimising the predetermined outcomes of educational selection as a fair rather than a fixed contest.

What underlies market policies is a number of ideological supports which assert that the state cannot successfully equalise educational opportunities through its attempts to standardise educational experience, and that the state monopoly of education is an infringement of individual freedom. The view that state intervention in education cannot generate greater equality of opportunity is supported by the assertion that there is a relatively small proportion of pupils who can benefit from an academic education due to differences in innate abilities and deep-seated cultural predisposition which, once formed, are largely impervious to change (Bantock, 1977). Moreover, as noted earlier, it is assumed that recent attempts to impose egalitarian ideals did so at the expense of standards of educational excellence. The educational system should therefore be exposed to free market forces, which will both allow a greater expression of parental choice, and also ensure that the system will be organised for the benefit of the consumers rather than the providers. Here we find the link between 'standards' and market solutions. The ideology of parentocracy therefore involves a significant change in political objectives, most important of which is the abandonment of educational policies geared towards generating 'equality of opportunity' (see Apple, 1989).

The deregulation and privatisation of schools shifts the responsibility for educational outcomes squarely on to schools and parents. If the school does not produce 'the goods' it is a poor school, and another should have been selected (assuming that a better alternative was available). Therefore if one's child does not perform and achieve to the expected level, then, as a parent, one must look to oneself for the reason. Perhaps it is because insufficient attention was given to the 'choice' of school, or perhaps some spare cash was spent on a holiday rather than invested in education. There is nothing morally wrong with the former course of action, it demonstrates consumer sovereignty, but of course it is no good looking to blame the state for personal decisions. One cannot have freedom without responsibility!

To summarise, it can be seen that the state has extended its control over the organisation and content of schooling in order to ensure that adequate educational standards are met. However, such intervention will stop short of ensuring that educational selection is based on 'equality of opportunity'. This 'selective minimalism' is justified on the grounds that egalitarian principles have already been tried and found wanting. Selection will now be determined by the free play of market forces, and because the state is no longer responsible for overseeing selection, inequalities in educational outcome, at least in official accounts, cannot be blamed on the state. Such inequalities (the right prefer the term 'diversity') will be viewed as the legitimate expression of parental preferences, differences in innate capacities, and a healthy 'diversity' of educational experience.

Underpinning much of the discussion in the present chapter has been the question of 'who shall be educated?' (Warner *et al*, 1946). However, this is not a question to be answered by the free play of market forces, because it is a political question concerning the distribution of knowledge, power and life chances. It is a question which also draws our attention to the role of the state in the production and reproduction of educational and social inequalities. This chapter barely touches upon these issues, but it does seek to offer some conceptual apparatus for beginning to think about the ideology of parentocracy in the third wave.

Note

This chapter is an abridged and modified version of 'The third wave: education and the ideology of parentocracy', *British Journal of Sociology of Education*, 11, 1 (1990), pp 65–85. The 'wave' analogy is taken from Toffler (1981).

References

Apple, M W (1989) 'How equality has been redefined in the Conservative restoration' in Secada, W G (ed) *Equality in Education* Lewes, Falmer Press.

Arnot, M and Weiner, G (1987) (eds) *Gender and the Politics of Schooling* London, Hutchinson.

Ball, S J (1993) 'Education markets, choice and social class: the market as a class strategy in the UK and the USA' *British Journal of Sociology of Education*, 14, pp 3–19.

Ball, S J and Larsson, S (1989) (eds) *The Struggle for Democratic Education: Equality and Participation in Sweden* Lewes, Falmer Press.

Bantock, G H (1977) 'An alternative curriculum' in Cox and Boyson (1977).

Belsey, A (1986) 'The New Right, social order and civil liberties' in Levitas, R (ed) *The Ideology of the New Right* Cambridge, Polity Press.

Bernbaum, G (1977) *Knowledge and Ideology in the Sociology of Education* London, Macmillan.

Botstein, L (1988) 'Education reform in the Reagan era: false paths, broken promises' *Social Policy*, 18, pp 3–11.

Bourdieu, P and Boltanski, L (1978) 'Changes in social structure and changes in the demand for education' in Giner, S and Archer, M (eds) *Contemporary Europe: Social Structure and Cultural Change* London, Routledge & Kegan Paul.

Bourdieu, P and Passeron, J C (1977) *Reproduction: In Education, Society and Culture*, London, Sage.

Bowles, S and Gintis, H (1976) *Schooling in Capitalist America* London, Routledge.

Brown, P (1987) *Schooling Ordinary Kids* London, Routledge.

Brown, P (1989) 'Education' in Brown, P and Sparks, R (eds) *Beyond Thatcherism* Milton Keynes, Open University Press.

Brown, P, Ainley, P and Scase, R (1994) *Degrees of Worth: the Rise of Mass Higher Education and the Decline of Graduate Careers* London, University College London Press.

Brown, P and Lauder, H (1992) (eds) *Education for Economic Survival: From Fordism to Post-Fordism?* London, Routledge.

Bulpitt, J (1986) 'The discipline of the new democracy: Mrs Thatcher's domestic statecraft' *Political Studies* 34, pp 19–39.

Cox, C B and Boyson, R (eds) (1977) *Black Papers 1977* London, Temple-Smith.

Cox, C B and Dyson, A E (eds) (1968) *Fight for Education* London, Critical Quarterly.

Dale, R (1985) (ed) *Education, Training and Employment* Oxford, Pergamon.

Dale, R (1989) *The State and Education Policy* Milton Keynes, Open University.

David, M (1980) *The State, the Family and Education* London, Routledge.

Deem, R (1978) *Women and Schooling* London, Routledge & Kegan Paul.

Dewey, J (1916) *Democracy and Education* New York, Macmillan.

Donald, J (1981) 'Green paper: noise of crisis' in Dale, R, Esland, G, Fergusson, R and MacDonald, M (eds) *Schooling and the National Interest* Lewes, Falmer Press.

Finn, D (1987) *Training without Jobs* London, Macmillan.

Flew, A (1987) *Power to the Parents* London, Sherwood Press.

Gallie, D (1988) (ed) *Employment in Britain* Oxford, Blackwell.

Gamble, A (1988) *The Free Market and the Strong State* London, Macmillan.

Green, D G (1987) *The New Right: The Counter-revolution in Political, Economic and Social Thought* Brighton, Wheatsheaf.

Halsey, A H, Floud, J and Anderson, C A (1961) (eds) *Education, Economy and Society* Glencoe, Free Press.

Harris, C C (1989) 'The state and the market' in Brown, P and Sparks, R (eds) *Beyond Thatcherism* Milton Keynes, Open University Press.

Hillgate Group (1987) *The Reform of British Education* London, The Claridge Press.

Hopkins, A (1978) *The School Debate* Harmondsworth, Penguin.

Hurt, J (1981) (ed) *Childhood, Youth and Education in the late Nineteenth Century,* Leicester, History of Education Society.

Johnson, R (1976) 'Notes on the schooling of the English working class 1780–1850' in Dale, R, Esland, G and MacDonald, M (eds) *Schooling and Capitalism* London, Routledge.

Jones, K (1989) *Right Turn: The Conservative Revolution in Education* London, Hutchinson Radius.

Lauder, H (1991) 'Education, democracy and the economy' *British Journal of Sociology of Education,* 12, pp 417–31.

Lauder, H, Middleton, J, Boston, J and Wylie, C (1988) 'The third wave: a critique of the New Zealand Treasury's report on education' *New Zealand Journal of Education Studies,* 23, pp 15–33.

Lauglo, J and Lillis, K (1988) (eds) *Vocationalizing Education: An International Perspective* Oxford, Pergamon.

Pahl, R (1988) (ed) *On Work* Oxford, Blackwell.

Parsons, T (1961) 'The school class as a social system: some of its functions in American society' in Halsey *et al* (1961).

Phillips, N R (1978) *The Quest for Excellence* New York, Philosophical Library.

Piore, M J and Sabel, C F (1984) *The Second Industrial Divide* New York, Basic Books.

Pring, R (1987) 'Privatisation in education' *Journal of Educational Policy,* 2, pp 289–99.

Purvis, J (1983) 'Towards a history of women's education in nineteenth century Britain: a sociological analysis' in Purvis, J and Hales, M (eds) *Achievement and Inequality in Education* Milton Keynes, Open University Press.

Sabel, C F (1982) *Work and Politics* Cambridge, Cambridge University Press.

Scruton, R (1984) *The Meaning of Conservatism* London, Macmillan.

Shilling, C (1989) *Schooling for Work in Capitalist Britain* Lewes, Falmer Press.

Shor, I (1986) *Culture Wars* London, Routledge.

Simon, B (1985) *Does Education Matter?* London, Lawrence & Wishart.

Simon, B (1988) *Bending the Rules: The Baker 'Reform' of Education* London, Lawrence & Wishart.

Tawney, R H (1931) *Equality* (reprinted 1983) London, George Allen & Unwin.

Toffler, A (1981) *The Third Wave* London, Pan Books.

Turner, R H (1961) 'Modes of social ascent through education: sponsored and contest mobility' in Halsey *et al* (1961).

Walford, G (1986) *Life in Public Schools* London, Methuen.

Warner, W L, Havighurst, R J and Loeb, M B (1946) *Who Shall be Educated?* London, Kegan Paul.

Whitty, G (1989) 'The new right and the national curriculum: state control or market forces?' *Journal of Education Policy*, 4, pp 329–41.

Wilby, P and Midgley, S (1987) 'The future of schooling lies with the Tory radicals' *The Guardian*, 23 July.

Wright, N (1983) 'Standards and the Black Papers' in Cosin, B and Hales, M (eds) *Education, Policy and Society* London, Open University Press.

Young, M (1961) *The Rise of the Meritocracy* Harmondsworth, Penguin.

Chapter 5

In Defence of Choice in Education

Brenda Almond

Parents, Education and the State

Modern states tend to regard the provision and control of education as both their obligation and prerogative. Instead of providing a framework for choice, they tend to look for some ideal model or blueprint for education, and to assume that once this has been found, it should be uniformly applied. Liberal democracies permit the existence of schools outside the framework of public provision, but this private sector, which varies in size in different countries, is nowhere as significant as the mainstream provision. Within the mainstream, only religious belief provides an exception to the general rule of pressure towards uniformity. Now there is something odd about this drive to a common education, since the states in question, whatever their particular political outlook, have joined in endorsing various declarations of human rights which are essentially incompatible with it, and which in fact give primacy to parents where education is concerned.

Two statements which make this presumption quite explicit are, first, within the framework of the Universal Declaration of Human Rights' assertion of the right to education:

> Parents have a prior right to choose the kind of education that shall be given to their children (26, 3)

and, in the International Covenant on Economic, Social and Cultural Rights, the undertaking to

> have respect for the liberty of parents and, when applicable, legal guardians to choose for their children schools, other than those

established by the public authorities, which conform to such minimum educational standards as may be laid down or approved by the State and to ensure the religious and moral education of their children in conformity with their own convictions.

There is a similar statement in the European Convention for the Protection of Human Rights and Fundamental Freedoms, ruling that:

In the exercise of any functions which it assumes in relation to education and to teaching, the State shall respect the right of parents to ensure such education and teaching in conformity with their own religious and philosophical convictions. (Article 2 of Protocol to the Convention)

As long, however, as consensus prevails on what should be the content and method of education and on how it should be organised, the implicit tension remains concealed. In the case of the United Kingdom, this tacit consensus prevailed for approximately two decades following the 1944 Education Act. Occasionally a case would arise which drew attention to the impotence of the individual dissenter in conflict with authority over some educational issue, but such cases were exceptional. It would have been natural to suppose that only cranks or extreme progressives would find themselves in any kind of confrontation with the state over their children's education. But following comprehensive reorganisation, there emerged an increasing number of cases in which parents who were dissatisfied with the arrangements offered them were prepared to keep their children away from school in an attempt to secure an education that met their wishes, rather than social needs as perceived by planners in central government or in local County Halls. A similar tension emerged in the United States in relation to a different issue: that of bussing to create racially mixed schools. Again, parents who put their own children's needs before what they may well have judged from every other point of view to be a worthwhile social and political objective, found themselves placed in the position of having to challenge the law. Finally, to take an example from continental Europe, students and parents in France showed themselves willing to flock to the streets to defeat government proposals to bring private schools under public control.

Now it is typical of parents – although of course no such generalisation is without exception – that they operate on a basis which is altruistic in the sense that they put their children's interests before their own, but is selfish in the sense that on the whole they put their own children's interests before those of others, or of the whole community. Although there are undoubtedly some people who place political or ideological principle before personal considerations, it would be generally true to say that most parents are not prepared to sacrifice their own children's welfare for the public good – this, even though they may be active in promoting arrangements that are bound in the short run to have comparable adverse effects for others.

Those who are consistent in applying their principles may, in any case, resist the suggestion that this is a sacrifice as far as their children are concerned, arguing that their children are likely to be ultimately advantaged by the transformation of society that is their goal. Even parents in this last category, however, may draw back in the face of a school phobic child, or a weeping child, or a bullied child. And indeed, casual observation suggests that those with an active interest in education who make a point of accepting the state choice and state arrangements for their children, usually place themselves in a position where that choice or direction is likely to be broadly acceptable, rather than in an area where the local school provides indiscipline, bullying and poor work goals. The state, by contrast, may seek to promote the public good, in a sense which is compatible with the sacrifice of some personal or individual interests.

This contrast is of considerable ethical and political importance. The central ethical issue is not, however, whether parents are hypocritical, or ought to be more consistent. It is, on the contrary, the more fundamental question of the legitimate boundaries of state power. This is not only a matter of the dominance of education in a modern state where, as in the United States, more than a third of the population may be involved in the education 'industry' at any one time as either consumers or suppliers. Nor is it simply a matter of the shrinking span in the lives of people in wealthy countries between the end of their own education and the start of their children's. Significant though these aspects are for anyone concerned with the totalitarian potential of education, there are two other features of education which affect the individual recipient even more directly. These are (a) that it is compulsory and (b) that it is time-consuming – this latter in the important sense that it consumes a child's years from infancy to the frontier of adult life. This means that if the state prescribes not merely education, but also where that education should take place, it becomes difficult to distinguish, at least in principle, between the case of a child in an ordinary educational establishment who must be in a specified place for fixed periods of time, and that of an electronically tagged prisoner whose movements are similarly controlled, or an offender committed to a progressive open prison with evening and weekend release.

From this point of view, then, education itself is an invasion of liberty. However, there is a paradox here, for it is also almost universally regarded as a prior *condition* of liberty by people of every political persuasion, from the anarchist left to the libertarian right. Both go on to infer from this the need for some state provision, although their suggestions as to the form this should take are radical. Milton Friedman, for example, offers a justification for at least a minimum of state provision in terms of the 'neighbourhood effect' of *not* providing compulsory education for those without personal resources. This, he argues, would be so adverse that self-interest alone provides a justification for it (Friedman, 1962, Ch 6). In terms of the argument from 'neighbourhood effect', without universal free education it is as impossible in the twentieth century for a well-off person to maintain a civilised standard of living in conditions of personal *security* as it was in the nineteenth century for such a person to live a *healthy* life without such public health measures as management of the water-supply and sewerage system. Not only may truancy itself be reflected in teenage crime, but educational failure creates the conditions for adult crime.

At the other end of the political spectrum, deschoolers, such as Ivan Illich (1971) and Everitt Reimer (1971), denounce the education system as it is to be found in developed Western countries as a tool of vested interests – a vast industry employing millions of people in a complex web of activities. Nevertheless, they do not reject education itself; they simply ask that educational resources be allocated on different principles. Their argument is not to be taken as a repudiation of the *need* for education but as a defence of a vastly different method of providing for it. Interestingly, both left and right converge in their practical recommendations: educational vouchers to be spent at choice by the consumer or recipient.

Who Speaks for Children?

If most people, then, are agreed on the need to constrain children's immediate freedom during the early years, for the sake of education, it is clear that at least in those early years, children are too young, too inexperienced, and above all, too infinitely malleable and adaptable, to determine the conditions and content of their education for themselves. Even those who advocate liberty most strongly see it as necessarily limited in the case of children. J S Mill, for example, in his classic defence of individual liberty, specifically excluded from the scope of the liberty principle 'children and young persons below the age which the law may fix as that of manhood or womanhood' (1954, p 73). Until recently, Mill's view would have been unchallenged by any serious thinker. Both Kant and Hegel, for example, had explicitly included the interests of the child within that of the male head of family; though the latter was concerned to correct Kant's approach to this issue to the extent of insisting that the members of a family retained their individual personhood, and were not regarded as mere 'things or instruments'.

That children themselves may have a perspective and should have a voice is a view of more recent origin and, not surprisingly, it is most often associated with thinkers concerned with educational practice. In particular, it has been 'child-centred' theorists such as Friedrich Froebel, John Dewey and A S Neill who have pressed the case for children's autonomy. But the kind of freedom in education promoted by these thinkers is an on-the-ground freedom – an adjustment of educational practice which nevertheless takes place within an assumed setting that has been provided by adults. More radical recent proposals for actually providing access to power for children themselves have been, for instance, suggestions that they be given the vote earlier (Harris, 1982), or that they should be allowed to reselect their own guardians or parental figures (Holt, 1974).

In the end, however, in the words of another group of commentators, proposals for child autonomy 'founder on the physical limitations of the youngest and most vulnerable' (Dingwall *et al*, 1983, p 91). It is for this reason that those who believe in personal liberty must see the child's interest at this stage as represented at first entirely by others, only gradually to be replaced with increasing autonomy of choice by the interests and claims of the child or school-age student. Since educational decisions must, and legitimately may, be made by others, whose is the ultimate authority in determining these decisions? It might be presumed that ultimate authority would lie with the child's parents, natural or adoptive. But professionals – teachers, social workers and others – are alternative claimants in a situation where government, too, may demand a say in decisions regarding children. So the stage is set for confrontation, or at least for controversy.

It is not difficult to find examples of conflict between parents, on the one hand, anxious to press the perceived interests of their children, and professionals – teachers, social workers – on the other, claiming the authority of expertise. When this kind of problem arises in the context of schools, the picture is further complicated by the fact that the goals of those in conflict may differ. In particular, they may be wholly educational or they may be non-educational. The ideal pattern may be imposed for its own sake – because it seems to represent the best form of education – or for the sake of such non-educational outcomes as social justice or equality. In either event a conflict is set up which falls within political party lines, with the ideology of liberalism (emphasising the freedom of the individual, toleration, and the right to be different) confronting the ideology of egalitarianism (emphasising the right of the state to enforce its preferred pattern on its citizens). This in itself justifies a differing moral perception of the imposition of patterns in the two cases.

Where objectives are clearly educational, the issue raised can be stated in terms of paternalism – that is to say, in terms of promoting the best interest of the child. But while there is general agreement that education is in children's interest, there is disagreement about what a good education is, and what it should achieve. One might compare Squire Brown's remark in *Tom Brown's Schooldays* – 'If he'll only turn out a brave, helpful, truth-telling Englishman, and a gentleman, and a Christian, that's all I want' – with the views of a contemporary working-class parent, who may want a child to be equipped with skills for the job-market, or with the views of a middle class intellectual who speaks of 'education for its own sake', or an educational progressive, who aims only to produce a happy child and a well-adjusted adult. There are also cultural and religious differences in present-day societies which affect educational aims. Even clearly educational objectives, then, do not produce unanimity.

But where the objectives are social objectives, the issue is no longer paternalism, with the attendant problems that entail as to what constitutes the child's best interest. It is rather a deeper political controversy about future patterns of society: should it be meritocratic and competitive, or egalitarian and welfare-oriented? Regulated or libertarian? Redistributive or laissez-faire? And since schools also serve to allocate social roles in a future society, there are still questions to answer even if the nature of that future society is agreed: of any one child or student it may be asked, how is she, or he, to participate either in that new society, or in society as it is presently constituted?

Disentangling the issues here is an understandably complex matter. One way to view it is as a triangle of competing interests, each claiming competing rights. At the centre of this triangle stands the child, at least until autonomy is reached (and this must be a continuous not a sudden process). The child is the object of competing claims by state, by professionals, and by parents, and it is a matter of considerable importance to assess the weight of these rival claims.

To begin with, each of the interested parties may present a moral claim. States or governments have always tended to claim the children within their borders as in some sense 'their own'. Plato, in his *Republic*, made such an assumption explicit, clearly setting the ties of family loyalty as in conflict with loyalty to the state, and setting out a pattern of education which depended on complete control of the experience and education of the child. Rousseau too, although he set out a highly individualised system of education in *Emile*, took a rather different view when he found himself in a position to influence practical policy. In his article on 'Political Economy' composed for the *Encyclopedie*, he wrote:

> If the reason of each individual is not allowed to be the sole judge of his duties, still less should the education of children be left to the ignorance and prejudices of their fathers ... The state abides: the family passes. (Boyd, 1962, p 41)

Where the claims of professionals, in particular teachers, are concerned, it is noteworthy that the emergence of this group as an influential body is a twentieth-century phenomenon. The contemporary explosion of knowledge has created the age of professionals – people, that is, who claim a prerogative based on superior knowledge, special training and on their professional relationship with their client. In the world of education, they may be particularly confident of their ability to control outcomes, given sufficient scope. As one psychologist, J B Watson, is reputed to have said: 'Give me that child until he is seven and I will give you the man' – a claim also made by another group traditionally associated with a high degree of educational control, the Jesuits.

The case for parents, by contrast, remains largely unargued in the contemporary setting, sentimental lip-service being given in their case to 'the good of the child' – a formula generally used to permit parents to make choices only so long as these conform to professional or political judgement. This has not always been so. Indeed, until recently, the assumption would have been that power in any decision-making relating to children must be exercised by parents. There was no paid army of professionals, and governments lacked the institutional, financial and bureaucratic apparatus to assert control. Nevertheless, parents have always had duties laid upon them in respect of their children, and it is arguable that duties presuppose rights. If, for example, parents are regarded as having an obligation to care for, instruct and protect their children, their right to do these things must be simultaneously recognised. It would be inconsistent to admit the 'ought' here, while withdrawing the 'can' – to demand fulfilment of the duty but to deny the practical conditions necessary for fulfilment of the duty. Or, as a contemporary British judge, Lord Fraser, has expressed this: 'From the parents' right and duty of custody flows their right and duty of control of the child' (quoted in Williams, 1985, p 1182). In the specific case of education, the British Education Act of 1944 was explicit in this respect. It ruled:

It shall be the duty of the parent of every child of compulsory school age to cause him to receive efficient full-time education suitable to his age, ability and aptitude, either by regular attendance at school or otherwise.

The phrase 'or otherwise' is highly significant, for it permitted a wide variety of educational arrangements, including private tuition and domestic education. Of course, if what parents want or decide is in the best interests of their child, their moral claim is greatly strengthened. However, parents can be misguided, and do not always do what is in the best interests of their child. This may seem to reduce the legitimacy of their claim. But the issue is complicated by the fact that in assessing the child's interest, an arbitrary judgement must be made as to when it should be calculated. The current under-16-year-old will later be a 20-year-old, a 30-year-old, a 40-year-old, and so on. It is common for a child's own wishes to be overruled just precisely in the light of some assessment of what the person at these later stages will then be likely to wish. Where education is concerned, it is assumed that the later person will wish for the benefits that accrue to those who have been educated – or at least wish to avoid the stigma that attaches to illiteracy and inability to earn a living.

Against a State Monopoly of Education

These, however, are minimal goals, and as long as disagreement is possible as to what the later person would desire and what is genuinely in the interest of the child, such considerations do not decide the issue in favour of the professional or the government rather than the parent. For governments and experts can be mistaken too, and in their case the potential damage that error can produce is on a vastly larger scale. This is the heart of the argument against educational monopolies, whether of experts or governments, or of experts working for governments. It is an argument for damage limitation, and at the same time an argument for social freedom in the widest possible sense. One author has put the point in the following terms:

> The practice of entrusting children to their parents ultimately limits the control of society to determine the life-style and beliefs of persons. (Schoeman, 1980, p 17)

It is because of the undoubted truth of this claim that totalitarian blueprints for society, from Plato's *Republic* on, tend to include an attack on the family as part of their proposals for political restructuring. There is no need to see the issue in political terms, however. The consequences are the same even when the motive involved is a disinterested, completely nonpolitical preference for the rule of experts as a way of securing the best possible management of children.

Parents, however, enjoy a unique advantage over experts: this is that their rule is not monolithic. There are as many ways of bringing up children as there are parents. It is also temporary: adult life brings with it exposure to competing viewpoints. Of course, experts too, and even governments, may not present a unanimous face. Indeed, they may change their opinions over time. The problem is, though, that the 'official' perspective, for as long as it is fashionable, tends to be imposed on everybody. But if this ubiquitous imposition were ever to be achieved on a substantial scale, there would be less scope for change and development, and, in particular, there would be no regression to the norm – something which fortunately appears to happen, on the whole, as a self-correcting mechanism where extreme educational theories are allowed to jostle for space with each other.

But utilitarian arguments – arguments based on assessing the personal and social impact of different ways of settling the question of who should make educational decisions – depend in the end on disputable matters of fact. It is therefore important to consider whether there are other arguments – in particular, arguments not based on paternalism – that might be advanced for assigning the controlling role to parents in children's lives, until they are ready to assume it for themselves.

One strongly nonpaternalist argument is that parents do, in a sense, have some claim to ownership of their children. Although not generally acknowledged, the strength of the feeling that this is so tends to be revealed frequently in tug-of-love cases between divorcing parents for the custody of their children. This proposition was expressed by Sir Robert Filmer, in his *Patriarcha* in these terms:

> the true and first reason of authority is that the father and mother, and simply those that beget and engender, do command and rule over all their children. (Laslett, 1959)

The idea that the biological relationship itself generates parental rights is of interest in itself, and is involved in the controversies that surround such issues as surrogacy, *in vitro* fertilisation and the transfer of gametes. These conflicts turn very directly on the differing weighting to be given to biological parenthood on the one hand, and social or nurturing parenthood on the other. It may reasonably be argued, however, that some qualified notion of at least temporary ownership does apply in the case of the parent-child relationship, and that this is linked, however conditionally, to the biological fact of generation. It may be that Hobbes was correct in seeing this as more like the right that people have to their own body than their right to ownership of property (1922, Ch 20). If so, the recognition of this right can only be intuitive, and cannot be founded on any consideration more compelling than it is itself. But whatever the force of the biological argument, it is clear that it cannot stand alone. It is worth turning, then, to some arguments for parental right which do not depend on this deep and intuitive, but nevertheless disputable, assumption.

Cultural and Religious Freedom

First amongst these is an argument from cultural and religious freedom. It is clear, to begin with, that there are persisting cultural disagreements as to the extent and limits of parental authority, and that some of these cultural disagreements are based on strongly held religious views. Some of the differences of opinion that this creates within a modern liberal state can be understood in terms of a requirement of toleration. There is a particular problem of toleration, however, when what is to be tolerated in one person affects the interest of another, whose preferences must ultimately be counted separately. And here it is arguable that if what parents desire on behalf of their child will produce some irreversible physical change (as it does, for example, in the case of female circumcision) then that absolute power of the parents must be limited by other agencies. But, of course, the issue of education is not so clear.

However, in general, once some necessary exceptions have been made, there is a strong *prima facie* case for the principle of cultural and religious freedom for people of mature years to carry with it a freedom for those same adult people to bring up their children according to their own beliefs, even if to others, perhaps even to the great majority, these beliefs seem in many ways irrational or misguided. Freedom of religion, then, together with freedom to maintain and perpetuate one's culture, provides one kind of independent argument – an argument, in other words, that is not linked to a judgement about the wellbeing of the child – for assigning ultimate authority in educational matters to parents.

A second kind of argument which is somewhat similar in its consequence is one based on moral rather than religious considerations. An argument of this sort is advanced by Ferdinand Schoeman, who argues that the right of parents to exercise power over their children is based on their own justifiable moral claim to a certain kind of intimate relationship. He writes:

Why should the family be given extensive responsibilities for the development of children? Why should the biological parent be thought entitled to be in charge of a family? I believe that the notion of intimacy supplies the basis for these presumptions. (1980, p 14)

Schoeman goes on to argue that intimacy requires privacy and autonomy as its setting, and that a parent's right to this type of private relationship overrides even some limited cost to the child. The focus of Schoeman's argument, then, is not the wellbeing of children, but the idea of close human relationships. For this reason he rejects the kind of argument advanced by Elizabeth Anscombe (1978) in which the legitimacy of an institution arises out of the fact that it is an institution carrying out an important task – an argument, that is, essentially based on utility. On this he comments:

> So long as families maintain their position of being necessary conditions for the performance of such functions, Anscombe's argument captures common sense and preserves family entitlements. But the emergence of alternative, possibly superior (relative to the child), means of rearing children would deprive the family of its position of being necessary and hence undermine its claim to rightful autonomy, except on a customary basis. (1980, p 13)

This conclusion is particularly important where education is concerned, for here the role of expert opinion may well be decisive. But education does not need to entail a vast centralised and bureaucratised statewide monopoly of all educational processes. In the last analysis education may be a personal and private enterprise without formal organisation. So the right of privacy is in fact of striking relevance here. It is only by respecting this right that it is possible to guard against the deep invasion of the personality which the compulsory and long-term nature of education would otherwise make possible. Abuse of the education process is something which has taken place under both fascism and communism and its prevention is central to the preservation of a free society. The positive ways in which this may be done may now be identified as:

1. Permitting individual families to opt out of the education system altogether on reasonable grounds, even while recognising the loss this may involve for the small number of children likely to be involved (growing up necessarily involves emancipation from

possessive or dominant parents, but no process of maturation can guarantee emancipation from a totalitarian state).

2. Permitting the existence of independent schools – not providing them with special subsidies, but not on the other hand creating unreasonable obstacles for those who choose to use them (even if their effect is socially distorting and the education they offer less than ideal, this is a smaller price to pay than the socially and politically distorting effect on society of a state monopoly of education).

3. Permitting individuals to perpetuate their own ideals and beliefs, particularly religious beliefs, through the family structure by retaining in their own hands ultimate control of the shape and direction of their children's education. This may involve the existence of schools of a particular religious persuasion, and again, while some might see it as preferable that children should not be indoctrinated in a particular religious belief – and some limits must obviously be set – it is even more important that an entire society should be preserved from the possibility of centrally controlled indoctrination either in religion or in anti-religion (for a further elaboration of these points by the present author, see Cohen, 1981).

This is an argument, however, for religious education which is funded and provided by either the individuals who want it, or the religious groups – churches, etc – who promote it. It does not provide a justification for the levying of money from the general taxpayers to support beliefs which may conflict with their own beliefs, values or ideological commitment. So in order to meet the requirement of religious freedom it is only necessary that a society should (a) permit the establishment of truly independent religious schools and (b) facilitate the limited withdrawal of children in state or publicly funded schools from ordinary lessons to receive special instruction at their parents' wishes.

Setting aside the special issue of religious education, the crucial point is that variety itself provides a check – a necessary dispersal of power. This raises a question about the size that schools should be; for clearly the maximisation of choice is related to the number and variety of alternatives available. If choice is to be maximised, schools should be as small as is consistent with efficiency. And in practical terms the development of a range of alternatives could be facilitated by a system of direct rather than indirect payment – the voucher system or some variant of it.

Finally, there is an argument – politically better known – of an economic nature. It is essentially the claim that choice produces *better* education. For if parents are free to choose their children's education, schools will be obliged to compete in providing the kind of education parents want. Many parents will have as goals certain standards of moral and social behaviour, and the 'market forces' argument is quite consistent with fostering goals of this sort. Its more distinctive application, however, is to economic and vocational objectives. If the objective of parents is in general their children's competence and subsequent employability, the 'market forces' argument is that schools will be *indirectly* obliged to provide the kind of education that society in general, and employers in particular, require. And more indirectly still, since what employers want is economic success and international competitiveness and viability, and since they need employees who can contribute to these ends, choice-based schools will in the end be schools that provide an education in the skills needed by a worker in a competitive market-based economy. The 'market forces' argument, then, is that schools that do not do this will go out of business as parents take their children – the school's clients – elsewhere. This argument finds nothing politically or ethically unacceptable about such indirect pressures and, indeed, it prefers them to direct intervention by government to pursue these or other ends. The 'market forces' strategy can operate, however, only in an open situation where information about schools and their performance is freely available. There may be a role for government, then, in ensuring that this necessary precondition exists. In sum, the principle that should guide a government which sets a high priority on liberty is that of leaving the ultimate determination of any child's individual experience to the maximum possible extent in the hands of the child's own family. Within schools, the aim should be to recognise and develop diverse talents and interests, rather than to attempt to produce a uniform product. Those who create a potential Frankenstein's monster in the shape of centralised state powers for education should not be surprised if in the future their creation takes on an unsought and unwelcome life of its own.

Note

I am grateful to Richard Smith, editor of the *Journal of Philosophy of Education*, for permission to use my article 'Education and liberty: public provision and private choice' *Journal of Philosophy of Education*, 25, 2 (1991), pp 193–202, as the basis of the present chapter.

References

Anscombe, E (1978) 'On the source of the authority of the state' *Ratio*, 20, pp. 1–28.

Boyd, W (1962) *The Minor Education Writings of Jean-Jacques Rousseau* NY Teachers' College, Columbia University.

Cohen, B (1981) *Education and the Individual* London, Allen & Unwin.

Dingwall, R, Eekelaar, J and Murray, T (1983) *The Protection of Children* Oxford, Blackwell.

Friedman, M (1962) *Capitalism and Freedom* Chicago, Chicago University Press.

Harris, J (1982) 'The political status of children' in Graham, K (ed) *Contemporary Political Philosophy* Cambridge, Cambridge University Press.

Hobbes, T (1922 [1651]) *Leviathan* London, Dent.

Holt, J (1974) *Escape from Childhood* Harmondsworth, Penguin.

Illich, I (1971) *Deschooling Society*, London, Calder & Boyars.

Laslett, P (ed) (1959) *Patriarcha and Other Political Works by Robert Filmer* Oxford, Oxford University Press.

Mill, J S (1954 [1859]) *On Liberty* London, Dent.

Reimer, E (1971) *School is Dead* Harmondsworth, Penguin.

Schoeman, F (1980) 'Rights of children, rights of parents, and the moral basis of the family' *Ethics*, 91, pp 6–19.

Williams, G (1985) 'The Gillick saga' *New Law Journal*, 29 November, p 1182.

Chapter 6

Parental Choice and Education for Citizenship

Patricia White

One can be a devout preacher, a courageous soldier, a dutiful patrician and a bad citizen.

J-J Rousseau (quoted by Shklar, 1990, p 13)

Can one be a good parent and a bad citizen? What is involved in being a good parent and a good citizen in a democratic society? The UK government in recent years has promoted parental choice in education and also the notion of citizenship and education for citizenship. But how far are there tensions between these two ideas? It is often claimed that parental choice of schools is very much in line with democratic values and the likely resulting diversity of schools is highly appropriate to a pluralistic democracy concerned to respect the values of minorities. This would suggest that parental choice of schools and citizenship education happily go hand in hand. Children go to schools chosen by their parents and are aware of the respect their society pays to the individual's values expressed in that choice. But what do they learn about choice and democratic citizenship, if, for instance, they go to exclusive private schools, rigidly hierarchical schools or schools based on a fundamentalist conception of obedience to a religious creed? In this chapter we examine what kind of parental choice of education is compatible with a robust notion of citizenship in a democratic society.

The Family in the Democratic Context

Parental choice cannot be discussed in a vacuum. As others (eg Blustein,

1982) have shown, the role and position of the family has been different in different historical contexts. Most immediately fruitful for the current debate is to look at the family within the democratic context and this involves at least a brief indication of what is to be understood by democracy. Democracy is clearly an idea involving a whole cluster of values – freedom, justice, the common good, respect for the individual – and therefore, as the shelves of libraries and bookshops testify, capable of myriad interpretations – maximal, minimal, representative, participatory – in part because of the possibility of assigning different weightings to those values. The tensions I have alluded to above, however, between parental choice and democratic values begin to emerge even if one works with a broad and reasonably uncontroversial notion of democracy. That notion would be of political arrangements which, in the interests of the personal autonomy of the individuals living within them, allow citizens, as of right, to participate in the control of political power, allowing this right, on the basis of justice, to all citizens, without discrimination. In more minimal conceptions of democracy this will take the form of control over elected representatives and, in more maximal conceptions, of direct participation in decision-making. Premised on the value of personal autonomy in this way, democracy protects citizens' rights to autonomy by securing the conditions for its emergence (for example, through education), its development, maintenance and exercise (for example, via freedom of expression). Democratic citizens do not plead with, request or beseech their rulers to enact policies or refrain from enacting them, as in former times subjects might have petitioned monarchs, but as holders of rights, they make justified claims on government.

Given this context, it is not surprising that we hear talk of parents' rights as part and parcel of the rights involved in being a citizen of a democratic society (see Fried, 1978; Strike, 1982; Crittenden, 1988). As Fried puts it,

> the right to form one's child's values, one's child's life plan and the right to lavish attention on the child are extensions of the basic right not to be interfered with in doing these things for oneself. (1978, p 152)

On this view, parental choice of education derives from the basic democratic right of citizens to personal autonomy, which, as I have indicated above, is the mainstay of the democratic idea. It is not clear, however, that parents *qua* parents have such a right. The core of the democratic idea, after all, is the right of *all* citizens to autonomy and to concede a parental right to determine the child's education in this way would be to privilege the parents' autonomy over the child's for no good reason, as a number of people have argued (for example, White, 1983, Ch 5; Gutmann, 1987, pp 28–33; Tamir, 1990).

What is the upshot then? If parents have no rights as parents over their children's education, does this mean that a democratic state has no place for a role for parents and family in the formation of its citizens? Equally, are parents who teach their toddlers not to snatch their friends' toys and try to influence their teenage children towards making responsible choices in sexual and other areas of their lives, infringing the autonomy of their offspring in some way offensive to their development as citizens? Would a truly democratic state have to dispense with parents and families?

To draw such an inference from the argument against parental rights would be wrong. There are several arguments for accepting the existence of parents and the family rather than some alternative (for example, communal) way of bringing up children. It can be argued (see White, 1983, Ch 5) that becoming a parent and bringing up a family is something that most people want to devote a part of their lives to and also something which brings them considerable satisfaction. That being so there is no reason to devise some other way of bringing up children unless they are manifestly harmed by being brought up within a family by natural or adopted parents. We do not need to talk the language of rights here and proclaim a right to procreate and rear. As Mary Midgley (1991) says:

> The reason why parents are taken to be normally the least bad available rearers for their children is not any belief about a particular right. It is widespread experience that other people are, almost always, much less willing even to try to do the job properly than the parents are ... Attempts to provide adoptive or institutional or foster-care rely on finding people to give it who will provide the enormous devotion the job demands, *and who do not share the faults of the parents.* (her italics).

Refusing to talk about parents' rights to procreate, rear and form their children's values is not then to give up the idea of upbringing within the family. That remains a demanding responsibility for parents and one which necessarily involves responsibility for part of the child's education. It must include the tasks of teaching children their mother tongue and at least their early moral education and also the task of helping them, until they can do this for themselves, to make coherent sense of the various educational experiences that come their way from different sources. If children are to be brought up within the family, this much must be done by parents. Given, then, this part in their children's educational development, are they not in a good position, if not indeed the best position, to choose the kind of school their child should attend? Let us examine two views which suggest that they are and that this is in line with democratic principles.

Is Parental Choice of School Compatible with Democratic Values?

The first view makes the modest claim that parental choice of school is *compatible* with democratic values. It is characteristically advanced to justify parents' rights to send their children to schools outside the state system. It does this by making reference to the principle of liberty, as a bedrock value in a democracy, and arguing that it is compatible with democratic values for parents to have the right to opt to send their children to independent schools (ie fee-paying schools which in the UK would include public schools). Parents, it is claimed, must be allowed to spend their money as they wish and that must include being allowed to spend it on their children's education. This argument is, however, inconclusive to say the least. Citizens in a democracy are prevented from spending their money on hard drugs and weapons, without appropriate licences, in the interests, *inter alia*, of the community as a whole. Perhaps the same kind of considerations should apply in the case of independent schools.

Whatever other qualities parents may want from a school, they should, as citizens as well as parents, want it, at the least, to be supportive of the democratic framework in which they are bringing up their children.

At the moment independent schools in the UK may not be supportive of democracy, even on a minimal account of democracy, where citizens have a certain civil status, associated with certain rights, within a community based on a rule of law and are expected to vote for representatives (cf Carr, 1991; McLaughlin, 1992). For there is no requirement on independent schools to teach a curriculum or maintain an ethos which is supportive of a democratic system. So that even the slender support for a democratic system that might be expected to come from the National Curriculum and the cross-curricular themes may not be available. It may be argued that independent schools are not required to do these things but that, as a matter of fact, they do. Even if true, that leaves the question of why what are judged to be the necessary knowledge, attitudes and skills of a democratic citizen should be optional for independent school students while required of other school students. It also follows that parents cannot take for granted an education supportive of even a minimal democracy.

However, even if independent schools *can* provide an education supportive of a minimal democracy, it is not clear that, in their present form in the UK, they can provide support for a more full-bodied democracy. This requires of citizens that, *inter alia*, they have some concern for the common good, an active concern for their fellow citizens and have some responsibility for participation in political decision-making. The socially divisive character of the independent school system in the UK would seem to work against this. For in the UK the public school system has meant that powerful positions in our society tend always to be occupied by a limited social group. Members of the government, governors and directors of the Bank of England and Church of England bishops come predominantly from public schools.

As well as the major issues of social justice to do with access to these positions, the question is often asked whether those who come to occupy them have the appropriate kind of experience of the social community they are to serve. Certainly people who have had such an education will have had no chance at school, in a face-to-face context, to develop bonds of trust with, and respect for, a whole range of fellow citizens. They will, at best, only be able to understand them at a distance. This seems to be a missed educational opportunity for education for citizenship in a pluralist, multicultural society. This point arises in a particularly strong form in connection with the second claim for parental choice in a democracy and therefore it makes sense to discuss its difficulties in considering that claim.

Does Parental Choice of School Further Democracy?

The second argument for parental choice of schools takes a stronger form (see White, 1988). It claims that parental choice is not merely compatible with the values of a pluralistic democracy, but rather better furthers the ends of such a democracy than a situation which does not allow for such choice (see O'Hear, 1987; Almond, 1991). Anthony O'Hear, for instance, has argued that it caters for the 'genuine flexibility and diversity in education that true liberals ought to cherish'. It allows diverse groups in our society, for instance Sikhs and Muslims, to establish their own schools rather than 'send their children to schools that can cater for them only imperfectly and by painful compromise'.

To view the likely consequences of parental choice (namely, separate schools for separate groups) in this light is, it seems to me, radically to misperceive the major problem facing democratic education in any pluralistic society. There are delicate balances to be struck in any such society between the shared life of citizens and the fostering of diversity. The diversity and variety of ways of life and practices must be matched by a strong sense on the part of citizens of the things they have in common as members of the same democratic society.

As many have argued, the survival of a democratic society depends on its citizens having an understanding of and commitment to democratic values and having democratic qualities of character: courage, integrity, honesty, trust, respect for others, self-respect and so on. This is not a matter of intellectual understanding alone, since the qualities of character are learned through living the democratic life alongside people in whom these qualities are second nature. Educational institutions need to embody in their practices both a recognition of the diversity and the bonds of mutuality connecting citizens. For toleration requires trust and the building of relationships of trust between groups is a delicate matter. It requires careful attention to the formation, maintenance and, should it be needed, the repair of such relationships (see White, 1993). This seems to indicate a need for common schools, run on democratic lines, where people grow to respect and trust each other and are concerned not merely to live and let live but that others should flourish. With the result that compromise is not regretted but welcomed as a way of accommodating others' concerns.

Separate schools, even following a national curriculum, might well tend to sharpen the differences between people at the expense of attention to society's internal cohesiveness and the need to develop common bonds between citizens. Young people growing up in monocultural schools would, I suspect, simply fail to develop common bonds with other groups in other schools. It is also likely that they would be inexperienced in the attitudes appropriate to, and skills necessary for, negotiation and compromise where these really matter.

When I think of the likely consequences of separate schools for different ethnic and religious groups, I am reminded of Mill's remarks in *Representative Government* about the interest of the excluded always being in danger of being overlooked. Mill is concerned with the representation of working class people in Parliament but his remarks can, I think, be seen as relevant to the issue of common schools or separate schools. For where in our society can young people learn to listen to other people's viewpoints? The school is the public institution where young people can be helped to learn the essential democratic practice of listening and trying to understand others' views. Mill, in a familiar passage, puts the point like this:

> in the absence of its natural defenders, the interest of the excluded is always in danger of being overlooked; and, when looked at, is seen with very different eyes from those of the persons whom it directly concerns ... does Parliament, or almost any of the members composing it, ever for an instant look at any question with the eyes of a working man? When a subject arises in which the labourers as such have an interest, is it regarded from any point of view but that of the employers of labour? I do not say that the working men's view of these questions is in general nearer to the truth than the other: but it is sometimes quite as near; and in any case it ought to be respectfully listened to, instead of being, as it is, not merely turned away from but ignored. (Mill, 1910, p 209)

The analogy is a fairly loose one. But if for employers of labour and working men we substitute 'the white majority' and 'ethnic minorities', or any other groups (for example, the able bodied and the disabled), in any combination, the force of Mill's point for education in a democratic society should make us think hard about the desirability of a system which is likely to lead to separate schools for different groups of citizens. People from minority and majority groups need to hear each other speaking with their own voices rather than some media-filtered, or even teacher-filtered, version of that voice. It is one thing to be told *about*

Muslims and their beliefs; it is quite another to work and play *with* Muslims in the framework provided by a common school.

It is hard to see therefore that parental choice, if it produced separate schools along ethnic and/or religious lines, would further a democratic society whose members were concerned, in any sensitive way, with the wellbeing of other citizens with, perhaps, some attitudes and values very different from their own.

Citizenship, Parental Choice and Separate Schools

It is important at this point to make five clarificatory points about the precise character of the case which has emerged.

First, this case is not concerned with the practical problems – for instance, the reality of choice outside of large cities – which can be raised about parental choice, but, as I said at the outset, with the possible tensions between this and education for citizenship in a plural society.

Second, the case is not against parental choice as such but against certain kinds of parental choice, namely that of separate schools for different groups.

Third, in the nature of things, the case against separate fee-paying schools or separate schools for some religious and ethnic groups, cannot be a logically tight one. It has to rest on claims which refer to 'likely consequences'. The likely consequences which have emerged, however, do not strain credulity. We have plenty of experience of our readiness to see groups we know little about as alien and from there it is a small step to making them scapegoats for some ill or other. Given human weakness for this line of thought we need to take extra care in our educational arrangements positively to counteract it.

Fourth, what is therefore emerging is a positive case for children to be educated within a common institution. That context offers a chance for children from all groups to be seen as three-dimensional people rather than shadowy 'others', who in some cases, for instance, have their outsider status marked by being falsely referred to as immigrants.

Finally, if there is no objection to parental choice of school *per se*, perhaps parents themselves could make educated choices which could take into account the demands of citizenship education. Let us therefore, in a final section, see whether parental choice of school could be relied on to produce an appropriate citizenship education.

Parents and Citizens: A Partnership

Amid all the current discussion, in the UK and many other parts of the world, about the benefits parental choice is alleged to bring, there seems not to be a single defender of unfettered parental choice in a democratic society. This is for the good reason that politicians and educational and philosophical commentators alike recognise that a democratic society cannot do without some form of common civic education (see, for example, Crittenden, 1988; Galston, 1989; Gutmann, 1989).

The full benefits of civic education, however, cannot be provided by parental choice of *school*, even if parents find a school which embodies democratic values of respect for others, tolerance and so on, in a caring environment, whose standards in academic, practical and aesthetic aspects of the curriculum are all they would want. For civic education must be community-wide. This is clear if what parents committed to democratic values really want for their children is re-examined. They do not simply want a school which, as well as providing an appropriately broad education, is, for instance, girl-friendly, or where children from minority groups feel at home, or where basic standards of decency are fostered; they want a *society* in which those things and the other democratic values obtain. To have a society like that, all schools need to offer civic education. This will include a common curriculum as well as, equally importantly, guidelines to which the organisation and ethos of schools must conform if they are to contribute to education for citizenship.

Unfortunately we in the UK do not have this situation as an arena for parental choice at present. Our current National Curriculum in England and Wales with its disparate subjects and add-on cross-curricular themes is not appropriate to the task. As a number of commentators (for example, O'Hear and White, 1991) have shown, it is woefully inadequate as a preparation for democratic citizenship. Its inadequacy stems in large measure from the lack of an underlying conception of what is required for democratic citizenship. In *A National Curriculum for All*, O'Hear and White offer a blueprint for an education which takes its aims from the qualities required for self-determined wellbeing in a democratic society, embedding, for instance, the knowledge and understanding required within the framework provided by those aims and recognising that the aims will be realised both through the timetabled curriculum and the ethos and organisation of the school. It is not necessary to accept this scheme in all its detail to acknowledge that something along these lines provides a more promising way to set about establishing the framework for a common civic education.

Given, however, that such a framework of common civic education existed, would there be any place for parental choice? Or has its seemingly all-pervasive character left no space for a parental say in the education of children? The provision of the common civic education attempts to ensure that the wellbeing of all children as members of a democratic society is catered for, but that must necessarily be in broad terms as a matter of social policy. Individual parents have the responsibility to ensure their particular child's wellbeing is being provided for. This will mean, for instance, in the first place choosing, from among the schools on offer, the one which, because of its size or on account of some other feature, best suits their child's particular psychological make-up. What may also be relevant in the initial choice of school is what it is offering beyond the common civic curriculum. Subsequently, taking parental responsibilities seriously will mean working with the school to provide the support the child needs to progress both academically and personally. It may also mean, on occasion, having to complain about inadequate provision on the child's behalf.

Will the schools on offer include private schools? If a private school provides the agreed common civic education, does not cater only for a certain social group – for instance, the rich, or those from a particular ethnic or religious background (since, as argued above, this would be likely to frustrate the aims of common civic education) – the democratic state would have no reason to prohibit it. There could then exist privately funded schools which both provided common civic education and were not religiously or otherwise exclusive (how this might be managed, via a voucher system or in some other way, is outside the scope of this chapter) and parents could choose whether or not to spend their money on them. How likely it is that such schools would be established, within these constraints, remains somewhat unpredictable.

In the UK today, without an adequate framework for a common civic education, the conditions necessary for good parents also to be good citizens leave something to be desired. In such circumstances those aspiring to fulfil both roles can only attempt in adverse circumstances to do their best in what may have to be an imaginative, but still not entirely satisfactory, matching of the needs of their child with the educational opportunities on offer. The conception of educational partnership developed here makes it rather easier for good parents to be good citizens.

References

Almond, B (1991) 'Education and liberty: public provision and private choice' *Journal of Philosophy of Education*, 25, 2, pp 193–202.

Blustein J (1982) *Parents and Children*, Oxford, Oxford University Press.

Carr W (1991) 'Education for citizenship' *British Journal of Educational Studies*, 39, 4, pp 373–85.

Crittenden B (1988) *Parents, the State and the Right to Educate* Melbourne, Melbourne University Press.

Fried C (1978) *Right and Wrong* Cambridge, MA, Harvard University Press.

Galston, W (1989) 'Civic education in the liberal state' in Rosenblum, N L (ed) *Liberalism and the Moral Life* London, Harvard University Press.

Gutmann A (1987) *Democratic Education* Princeton, Princeton University Press.

Gutmann, A (1989) 'Undemocratic education', in Rosenblum, N L (ed) *Liberalism and the Moral Life* London, Harvard University Press.

McLaughlin, T H (1992) 'Citizenship, diversity and education' *Journal of Moral Education*, 21, 3, pp 235–50.

Midgley, M (1991) 'Rights talk will not sort out child abuse: comment on Archard on parental rights' *Journal of Applied Philosophy*, 8, 1, pp 103–14.

Mill, J. S. (1910 [1861]) *Representative Government*, London, Dent.

O'Hear A (1987) 'Taking liberties', *Times Educational Supplement*, 16 January.

O'Hear, A and White, J (1991) *A National Curriculum for All: Laying the Foundations for Success*, IPPR Education and Training Paper No 6.

Shklar J (1990) *The Faces of Injustice* London, Yale University Press.

Strike K (1982) *Liberty and Learning* Oxford, Martin Robertson.

Tamir Y (1990) 'Whose education is it anyway?' *Journal of Philosophy of Education*, 24, 2, pp 161–70.

White P (1983) *Beyond Domination: An Essay in the Political Philosophy of Education* London, Routledge.

White, P (1988) 'The New Right and parental choice' *Journal of Philosophy of Education*, 22, 2, pp 195–200.

White, P (1993) 'Trust and toleration: some issues for education in a multicultural democratic society' in Horton, J (ed) *Liberalism, Multiculturalism and Toleration* London, Macmillan.

Chapter 7

The Scope of Parents' Educational Rights

Terence H McLaughlin

Few would deny that parents have an important role to play in the upbringing and education of their children. But what is the nature and scope of the moral rights they possess in relation to these matters?

The area of dispute and disagreement regarding this question within contemporary educational, political and philosophical debate is wide. It is marked by two poles within which most discussion is conducted. To sketch matters roughly, at one pole is a general view which sees, within minimal limits, parental rights in education as fundamental, overriding and extensive. On this view (which for ease of reference I shall describe as the 'Parents as Determiner' view) there is a suspicion of the priority of 'professional' or 'political' judgement in educational matters and of a common form of education provided by the state. The child's educational experience is seen as properly determined to the greatest possible extent by the child's own parents and family. At the opposite pole is a general view which I shall describe as the 'Parents as Trustee' view. On this view, it is denied that parents *qua* parents have any rights over their children's upbringing and education independent of the duties they have in relation to these activities. One of the most basic of these duties is to enable their children to become rationally autonomous persons and democratic citizens. The fundamental rights at issue on this view are those of the children, which are merely 'held in trust' on their behalf by parents. This view is suspicious of parental choice of school as straightforwardly conducive to the satisfaction of these parental duties, and favours children being educated together within common schools.

These two poles of argument are recognisable, at least in general outline, as prominent features in contemporary debate. The contributions of Brenda Almond and Patricia White in this volume can be seen as representative examples of the first and the second poles of argument respectively. In this chapter, I shall explore some philosophical aspects of contrasting sets of views of these kinds and the conflict between them. I shall also outline my own general approach to the questions at issue. Although my exploration reveals unacknowledged complexity and does not aspire to offer a definitive resolution of the matters in dispute, I hope that it will contribute to contemporary debate by drawing attention to important considerations and lines of argument which are often neglected.

Preliminary Points

It is necessary to raise two preliminary points. First, despite the wide ranging disagreement which has been alluded to, it is important to note that there are areas of agreement in the debate. It is widely acknowledged, for example, that parents have *some* rights over their children's education and upbringing, even if these rights are seen, on occasion, as merely the correlative of wide-ranging parental duties. It is also generally recognised that parental rights cannot be *unlimited* and *absolute*. At the very least, parents do not have a right to inflict a manifestly cruel and abusive form of upbringing upon their children. Parents' rights are therefore limited by the rights and 'best interests' of their children, although views differ on precisely how these are to be construed. Another source of limitation on parents' rights, as Ruth Jonathan has emphasised, springs from the rights and needs of other parents and of society generally (Jonathan, 1993). This is also widely agreed in principle although, again, there is much dispute about how this source of limitation is to be characterised and evaluated.

A second important preliminary point concerns the distinction between justifications of parental rights on grounds of *principle*, and justifications on *practical* grounds. One may disagree that parents have certain *moral* rights, but concede that, for various reasons, equivalent *legal* rights cannot be denied as a matter of practical policy. For example, although parental moral rights to choose independent fee-paying schools may be objected to on principle, it may have to be accepted in a given context that it is politically very difficult or impossible to abolish such schools and parental legal rights related to them. There is an important difference between the two levels of justification. To establish parental moral rights at the level of principle is to provide a fundamental justification and a target to be achieved in legal terms as far as possible given practical realities. To establish parental legal rights on practical grounds is to accomplish less, at least from a philosophical point of view.

In this chapter, I shall concentrate upon matters of principle. It is important to note, however, that in regard to the rights of parents, questions of principle and practice are not easy to distinguish. Any adequate discussion of parental rights cannot avoid making a number of empirical assumptions and judgements and this is necessary for the full articulation of relevant principles. In attempting to confine my attention to matters of principle, I do not overlook this complexity but seek to achieve a greater clarity on fundamental matters.

The 'Parents as Determiner' View

Such views often claim that they give a high priority to liberty. It is clear, however, that it is the liberty of *parents* which is primarily emphasised. Arguments of this kind invite two broad criticisms relating to the limitations on parental moral rights noted above; those relating to: (a) the rights and 'best interests' of the child and (b) the rights and needs of other parents and of society. I shall examine each of these in turn.

The rights and 'best interests' of the child

This general position usually adopts a fairly minimalistic view of what the rights and 'best interests' of the child, as distinct from those of the parent, consist in. The necessary limits of parental rights in upbringing are often drawn, for example, in relation to such practices as ritual mutilation and domestic slavery. In education, these limits often refer to such matters as a failure to provide for the development of basic literacy and numeracy or to avoid what Coons and Sugarman describe as 'the scholastic equivalent of booze' (Coons and Sugarman, 1978, p13).

There is no sustained acknowledgement and development of the point that the child's rights and 'best interests' may involve something much fuller than this: the achievement of a significant form of autonomy.

The essential notion here is described by Joel Feinberg (1980) as 'the child's right to an open future', a right of children to reach maturity 'with as many options, opportunities, and advantages as possible' (p 130). This, claims Feinberg, is the fundamental 'best interest' of the child which parents have a duty to facilitate and which acts as an important limitation on their rights. It involves (for example) their avoiding the foreclosure of options for children through the making of certain 'crucial' and 'irrevocable' decisions determining the course of lives at too early a stage (p 143) and a requirement that children be provided with a broad education which acquaints them with 'a great variety of facts and diversified accounts and evaluations of the myriad human arrangements in the world and in history' (p 139).

This account of the rights and 'best interests' of the child is a central aspect of Patricia White's view, among others (see also, for example, Ackerman, 1980, Ch 5). The view is a complex one, and needs to be carefully understood. It acknowledges, for example, that such a 'sophisticated autonomy right' cannot be fully exercised by children until later points in their development, hence the notion that the parent has a duty to act as a 'trustee' of it. The view also acknowledges that parents can and should provide an initial 'primary culture' for a child (ibid) but stresses that, in various ways, parents must ultimately 'take their chance' with external influences (Feinberg, 1980, p 140). It is also important to note that, typically, the ideal of autonomy is located within, and is to be understood in relation to, the notion of a liberal democratic society and its principles, values and characteristics.

Properly understood, this conception of the rights and 'best interests' of the child presents itself as a significant limitation, at least in principle, upon parental rights. Although, as I shall acknowledge later, the conception is not without its difficulties, the claim that the 'best interests' of the child involves more than the minimal account indicated above seems intuitively plausible.

This may explain why detailed arguments by particular thinkers for extensive parental rights often contain in their treatment of the child's rights and 'best interests' an apparent commitment to the 'autonomy' conception, although this is not fully brought to bear on their arguments for parental rights.

Thus Brenda Almond (writing as Brenda Cohen) finds 'compelling' the aim that children 'should be allowed to mature into independent adults with their own view of life' (Cohen, 1981, p 34). She also seems to commit herself explicitly to the development of the autonomy of the child as being of fundamental importance in a liberal society (ibid, Ch 8). For example, she writes:

> there is a clear implication of liberal thought that the first condition for education in a free society – one based on tolerance and individual self-determination – is that it should be critical rather than conformist, and that it should aim at individual autonomy rather than social control. (p 81).

Thus, she claims, education must involve the development of capacities of 'rational thought' and 'critical appraisal' (ibid), respecting the 'essential freedoms of spirit' involved in areas such as morals, religion and politics; be broad in character; satisfy conditions relating to the education of women; respect academic freedom, and so on. Here Almond affirms that 'self-determination' and 'autonomy' are amongst the 'primary values' of liberalism (p 84).

But if these *are* primary values, and they have the implications for education in a liberal society which Almond indicates, then they must play a crucial role in the nature of the moral rights that parents can be allowed to claim in relation to that education (and in relation to their children generally). How can these values be rendered compatible with the extensive parental rights she favours? For surely more is required for the development of 'independent' adults than the rather passive process of 'allowing them to mature'. What of the significance here of planned educational experiences which parents have a duty to secure for their children?

Almond shares this difficulty with other writers seemingly committed to both the value of autonomy and wide-ranging parental rights. Coons and Sugarman (1978), for example, state that a crucial criterion in assessing the adequacy of a child's upbringing is whether it helps him or her to 'accumulate the stuff of self-determination' (p 2), a goal they describe as their 'primary objective' (p 71) and as 'an indispensable intellectual and ethical ideal' (p 72). Coons and Sugarman also acknowledge that the educational conditions required for the development of autonomy require 'more than minimums', but rather an 'exposure to and dialogue with issues of justice and personal morality' (p 76) and the drawing of the child into 'that human exchange about the nature of the good life which in large measure is the central subject of the permanent debate among a democratic people' (ibid).

It is hard, however, to reconcile these elements of Coons and Sugarman's argument with the wide-ranging parental rights which emerge on their account, and which includes the right (given only basic constraints) to choose a school promoting a particular 'world view' or conception of the good, including one based on the thoughts of Chairman Mao (p 10). There is no attempt to propose even principled constraints on these rights arising from the commitments described above.

The rights and needs of other parents and of society

Two prominent elements in this general category of limitation are those relating to social justice and to the requirements of preparation for life in a liberal democratic society.

On the former, 'Parents as Determiner' views are either suspicious of egalitarianism (see Cohen, 1981, Chs 2–3) or seek to reconcile wide-ranging parental choice with acknowledged demands of an egalitarian flavour by proposing such strategies as a 'constrained voucher system' (see Coons and Sugarman, 1978, Part IV, especially Ch 11).

With regard to preparation for life in a liberal democratic society, there is a tendency to underplay the fact that education is a public as well as a private matter. Almond accepts that 'today's schools are tomorrow's society' (Cohen, 1981, p 2), and that therefore 'in the shaping of the education system lies the shaping of the future political and social order' (p 71). In her description of this order, however, Almond says little about a *democratic* as distinct from a *liberal* society, but in places does acknowledge that it involves a 'sophisticated and highly participatory form of political life' (p 79), of which the free availability of education is 'an essential aspect'.

Yet she assigns a residual role to the state in education, equivalent to the duty of other members of society acting collectively to take the place of parents failing to provide basic care and nourishment. She gives as an example here a group of neighbours rescuing a child from the risk of death at the hands of a violent parent, or educating and caring for a child whose parents are dead (p 31). Despite her remarks elsewhere about the character of education in a liberal society she does not conclude that this generates the notion of an educational entitlement for all children, which, at least in principle, should not be frustrated by parental wishes. Almond also says little about the sort of education for democratic citizenship (a form of 'common civic education') emphasised by White and, indeed, excludes political teaching from schools (p 54). It is not clear how this approach can adequately shape through education a future liberal democratic political order of the sort indicated by Almond.

A similar point is made against Coons and Sugarman by Gutmann, in her claim that their proposals for education are inadequate with respect to the development in students of 'deliberative character' which she sees as the core political purpose for students of school age in a democracy (Gutmann, 1987, pp 50–52; 64–70).

Implications and conclusions

The 'Parents as Determiner' view may make a number of familiar responses to the criticisms which have been outlined. Some of these are predominantly practical in character. Claims in this category include the following:

1. that, as a matter of fact, it is both unwise and politically impossible to interfere with parental wishes because of the difficulties and consequences (intended and unintended) of the intervention;
2. that the alternatives have their own inherent dangers, not least those arising from the enhancement of the power of the state in educational matters; and
3. that a 'market' system of schooling is likely to produce, for various reasons, a better overall outcome in educational terms.

Points such as these require extensive discussion. A number of brief points can, however, be made about each.

Claim 1 involves the distinction made earlier between moral and legal rights. To reiterate the point made earlier, one may concede for various reasons that certain legal rights ought to exist without accepting that a principled basis has been provided for regarding them as moral rights. The 'Parents as determiner' view can be read in part as an account of the limit not of ideals but of legitimate intervention to secure their realisation.

The other two arguments require assessment in relation to neglected matters of principle. With regard to 2, for example, Almond's wariness about giving the state a more substantial responsibility for education derives in part from her unduly restrictive conception of what such state responsibility would involve. Throughout her argument, she often assumes that 'the state' is necessarily totalitarian in character, and gives insufficient consideration to the possibility that it could be a *democratic* one, subject to familiar democratic controls and concerned through its education system to promote not a determinate 'correct perspective' on controversial matters but the liberal values of personal autonomy and democratic citizenship. Perhaps parental indoctrination is preferable to state indoctrination, but this is not the only alternative.

With regard to 3, the argument that economically empowered parental choice produces a better education is one that requires evaluation in the light of a clear sense of the criteria of value to be invoked. Much further argument would be required to show that a market system of education can bring about an adequate form of education judged, for example, by the criteria invoked by Almond and by Coons and Sugarman referred to above. The notion that 'higher order values' relevant to education and schooling should be exempt from market forces requires serious consideration.

Other responses to the criticisms may have a more principled character. One of the most central of these concerns the 'autonomy' conception of the rights and 'best interests' of the child. While the intuitive plausibility of the conception is revealed by its presence in the views of the writers we have been considering, further (interrelated) questions concerning the precise meaning, significance and justification of the conception remain. On the question of meaning, defenders of the 'Parents as Determiner' view may claim that the conception is too imprecise and unclear to serve as an ideal of any substance in limiting parental moral rights. On the question of significance, it may be urged that, even if the problems of meaning could be overcome, there is room for considerable principled controversy about the implications that can be drawn from the conception for such rights; there may, for example, be many different ways in which autonomy can be developed. The question of justification may give rise to the claim that the conception is not a universal ideal applicable to all parents. Some parents may legitimately reject it. This is the position of Coons and Sugarman, who, despite their commitment to the conception elsewhere in their argument, ultimately, and without supporting argument, present it as '[merely] a personal view' (1978, p 71).

These complex questions are at the heart of any attempt adequately to delineate parental educational rights. I shall return to them shortly. While, as I shall later concede, some of the points made in relation to these questions by defenders of the 'Parents as Determiner' view have force, it is by no means clear that without a great deal of further argument they establish a principled defence of this perspective.

The 'Parents as Trustee' View

This pole of the argument gives full weight to the two sources of restriction on parents' rights neglected by 'Parents as Determiner' views. Thus parents are not seen as having moral rights which infringe the rights of their children to achieve autonomy and formation as democratic citizens. Education is seen as a Rawlsian 'primary good' for the child (see, for example, White 1983, pp 11, 38–39; Ch 3) which is justifiably subject to 'considerable control' by democratically determined national guidelines to ensure its adequacy and just availability to all children. Nor do parents have the moral right to make educational choices for their children which infringe the rights and needs of other parents or of society (through, for example, choosing schools which are socially divisive or unsupportive of democracy in other ways). A strong feature of arguments of this kind is that the requirements of education for democratic citizenship demand common schools.

Such views do not deny that practical considerations must be brought to bear on them. White, for example, recognises that highly relevant to her argument are judgements about the way in which educational institutions actually operate. She also acknowledges that, as a matter of fact, we live in an imperfect democracy and we lack an adequate framework for a common civic education. In this situation, parents are confronted with making decisions which involve dilemmas and unsatisfactory compromises on the basis of contextual judgement. This is relevant to the legal rights of parental choice which should exist in our current situation (see White, 1983, pp 155–57). Leaving aside such practical matters, what can be said of the view at the level of principle?

Relevant here are the questions about the meaning, significance and justifiability of the 'autonomy' conception of the rights and 'best interests' of the child which were raised at the end of the last section. Many versions of the 'Parents as Trustee' view assume that confident answers can be given to these questions. It is not clear, however, that sufficient attention is always given to complexities inherent in these issues.

For reasons of space, in illustrating this I shall concentrate on questions of the significance of the autonomy conception, and leave to one side questions of meaning and justification. For the purposes of argument, therefore, I shall assume that the 'autonomy' conception can be given coherent meaning and shall not discuss the fundamental difficulties that arise from parents and communities who explicitly do not value the autonomous life (see, for example, McLaughlin, 1992b; Fitzmaurice, 1993).

Even if we accept that the 'autonomy conception' is a coherent and justifiable ideal, its significance is called into question by considerations about how children achieve it. As was mentioned earlier, the role of a 'primary culture' provided by parents – an initial determinate and stable context of belief, practice and value – is an important element in this process. Children do not become autonomous in a vacuum. It is from such a determinate 'starting point', and from continuing conditions of stability as well as openness, that this development proceeds. This general point can be read into White's account of the duties of parents to teach children their mother tongue, to provide them with early moral education and to act as coordinators and monitors of their overall educational development to help them to make sense of the various experiences they are receiving from various sources.

A crucial question concerns the legitimate 'thickness' and extent of this 'primary culture'. White, for example, is concerned that parents might transmit 'some very particular conception of the good life' (1983, p 147) which would infringe the principle that there are no experts on the good life and frustrate the development of autonomy. This leads to her suspicion of religious upbringing and her view (roughly expressed) that religion is for consenting adults (1983, pp 146–47), a view mirrored in other writers who explicitly rule out religious upbringing on grounds of incompatibility with the 'autonomy conception' (Callan, 1985; Gardner, 1988). However, whilst manifestly indoctrinatory forms of upbringing are indeed incompatible with this conception, some thinkers are guilty of extending the boundaries of incompatibility too far. They seem to have a 'thin' notion of the sort of primary culture that can be provided by legitimate parental rights and an overconfident view of how 'appropriate non-particularity' in upbringing can be identified.

A similar point, arising from an underemphasis on the role of a settled context of belief, practice and value for the development of autonomy and liberal democratic citizenship, can be made about the emphasis placed by the view on common schooling. The implications of both of these points are outlined below.

The Scope of Parents' Educational Rights: Towards an Adequate Account

The discussion so far has accepted in broad terms the significance of limitations on parental rights emerging from the 'autonomy conception' of the rights and best interests of the child and from a liberal democratic conception of the rights and best interests of other parents and society. However, the 'Parents as Trustee' view stands in need of enrichment by an acknowledgement of the significance of a plurality of different ways in which these can be achieved.

In my view parents have wider moral rights in the provision of a 'primary culture' than is sometimes conceded. They extend, for example, to the right to provide certain forms of religious upbringing which can form one of the alternative bases from which the development of autonomy can proceed. A number of different forms of upbringing, including an introduction to 'thick' conceptions of the good, are compatible with the autonomy conception. (For references to recent debate on religious upbringing, including discussion of compatibility with autonomy, see McLaughlin, 1992b, n 27.)

With regard to schooling, I consider that there is a stronger argument for parental choice of school within the 'parents as trustee' perspective than is commonly recognised. White argues that all schools should offer education for democracy (a common civic education) with the implications for curriculum, organisation and ethos which she specifies. Separate schools explicitly rejecting this are clearly incompatible with her position. But might certain kinds of separate school be compatible? In addition to the common school, the importance of which is not denied, there may be a number of different schooling contexts in which the demands of openness and stability in the conditions required for the development of autonomy can be variously balanced, and in relation to which parents have moral rights of choice. One of these contexts might be separate schools seeking to provide both common civic education of an appropriate sort and a distinctive starting point for the growth of autonomy from the basis of a non-restrictive but sustained experience of a particular 'world view' or cultural identity, as in a 'liberal religious school' (for a fuller discussion of this claim, see McLaughlin, 1992b). The rights of parents to choose such schools can be justified in relation, for example, to an extension of the duties of monitoring and coordination of the educational experience of their children assigned to parents by White. Some parents may wish their child's education to proceed in a close relationship with the values and beliefs of the family. Given satisfaction of the demands of openness (see McLaughlin, 1992b) such a motive is compatible with the 'Parents as Trustee' view.

A major argument which White deploys against such a possibility is that pupils must encounter diversity face-to-face, as in the common school, rather than in the rather hypothetical way that is likely in a separate school. While this point has force, it must be judged alongside other considerations, only some of which can be indicated here. White concedes that 'delicate balances' need to be struck in a liberal democratic society between the 'shared life of citizens' and the 'fostering of diversity' (see also McLaughlin, 1992c). These balances need to be recognised in schooling arrangements also, and the sound motives which parents may have for these choices require recognition. Some parents, for example, may favour a 'liberal religious school' for the reason mentioned above, or because it facilitates the exposure of their children to a view of life which may be under threat in the wider society. The complexity of liberal values themselves also leads to doubts about whether an unproblematic set of ethical and other principles for the conduct of the common school can be specified from within this perspective (see McLaughlin, 1992a,b). While this does not constitute the fundamental educational disagreement often referred to in 'Parents as Determiner' views, it does lead to the acknowledgement of a legitimate plurality in forms of liberal education and schooling, against which the various benefits of the common school need to be weighed.

My general perspective enables a more sensitive judgement to be made about how the different considerations relevant to the scope of parental rights can be balanced. Unlike in the 'Parents as Determiner' view, the cultural and religious freedom of parents and their non-paternalistic interest in their children are not given free rein, but can be given greater salience than in many treatments of the 'Parents as Trustee' view through an acknowledgement of the more extensive moral rights parents have to provide, as a starting point for the development of the autonomy of their children, an initial determinate 'primary culture', and by extension a determinate form of schooling, harmonious with the values and beliefs of the family.

My discussion has been necessarily a limited one. It has been possible to deal with only certain principled aspects of the matters under consideration and many important issues have remained unexplored, not least the full character and justification of the parental rights which emerge on my own account. I trust, however, to have illuminated a line of argument which will, by counteracting a tendency to polarised debate on this issue, enable an appropriate and nuanced judgement of the legitimate scope of parents' educational rights to be made.

References

Ackerman, B (1980) *Social Justice in the Liberal State* New Haven, Yale University Press.

Callan, E (1985) 'McLaughlin on parental rights', *Journal of Philosophy of Education*, 19, 1, pp 111–18.

Cohen, B (1981) *Education and the Individual* London, George Allen & Unwin.

Coons, J E and Sugarman, S D (1978) *Education by Choice: the Case for Family Control* Berkeley, University of California Press.

Feinberg, J (1980) 'The child's right to an open future' in Aiken, W and LaFollette, H (eds) *Whose Child? Children's Rights, Parental Authority, and State Power* Totowa, NJ, Littlefield, Adams & Co.

Fitzmaurice, D (1993) 'Liberal neutrality, traditional minorities and education' in Horton, J (ed) *Liberalism, Multiculturalism and Toleration* London, Macmillan.

Gardner, P (1988) 'Religious upbringing and the liberal ideal of religious autonomy', *Journal of Philosophy of Education*, 22, 1, pp 89–105.

Gutmann, A (1987) *Democratic Education* Princeton, Princeton University Press.

Jonathan, R (1993) 'Parental rights in schooling' in Munn, P (ed) *Parents and Schools: Customers, Managers or Partners?* London, Routledge.

McLaughlin, T H (1992a) 'Fairness, controversiality and the common school' *Spectrum*, 24, 2, pp 105–18.

McLaughlin, T H (1992b) 'The ethics of separate schools' in Leicester, M and Taylor M (eds) *Ethics, Ethnicity and Education* London, Kogan Page.

McLaughlin, T H (1992c) 'Citizenship, diversity and education: a philosophical perspective' *Journal of Moral Education*, 21, 3, pp 235-250.

White, P (1983) *Beyond Domination* London, Routledge & Kegan Paul.

Chapter 8

Choosing Schools – The Consumers' Perspective

Anne West

During the last decade, the issue of choice of school has been addressed in a growing number of research studies in the UK, and indeed in the rest of Europe (Ballion and Oeuvrard, 1991).

As Andy Stillman has shown in Chapter 2, interest in the area of choice, particularly in relation to secondary schooling, has been ongoing for a number of years, but the Education Reform Act 1988 in England and Wales has added a new dimension to the issue. In theory, the Education Reform Act has altered the balance of power between parents and schools, with parents now having more say. In practice, however, the degree of choice varies considerably, depending on such factors as where parents live, how many schools are available within easy reach, whether schools are oversubscribed or not, and on schools' or local education authorities' admissions policies. Moreover, although policies on choice have 'tended to assume that all parents can exercise their choices equally' (David, 1993), there is evidence that other factors will determine how effectively 'choices' are made, such as awareness of schools' admissions policies and parents' knowledge of 'how the system works' (see West et al, 1993).

In this chapter factors relating to choice of primary, secondary and private schools are explored; the focus is on the choice of the parents, but the child's involvement in the process is also examined. The review is selective, with a particular emphasis on recent quantitative research studies that, in addition to investigating factors important in the choice process, have also explored differences among specific groups of parents. A number of other studies have been recently reviewed and analysed by David (1993).

Parental Choice of School

Primary school choice

Relatively few studies examining how parents choose primary schools have been carried out. The studies reviewed all include an examination of factors parents considered in relation to their choice of a primary school for their child.

Although the education system in Scotland is different from that in England and Wales, it is worth examining the findings from a major research project carried out in Edinburgh (see Adler *et al*, 1989), as it is one of the largest of its type that has been carried out in the United Kingdom. The study involved interviewing 410 parents who had a child due to start primary school. As part of this study, parents were asked what the four most important reasons were for wanting their child to attend the 'requested school' as opposed to the 'catchment' area school. Parents who had not considered a school other than the catchment area school were not asked about their choice. Differences emerged between parents' views in the three different geographical locations examined. The most frequently mentioned factors varied but several consistently emerged in all three locations – namely, the child's happiness, proximity and siblings attending the school.

More recently, Hughes *et al* (1990) interviewed 141 parents in the south-west of England. As part of this study they were asked why they had chosen their child's primary school. A wide range of responses emerged. The key reason was the school's locality (mentioned by 79 per cent) – namely that it was easily accessible from the child's home. Two-thirds of the parents made reference to the school's reputation or that it had been recommended. Over a third of the parents (38 per cent) had been impressed by the school when they had visited.

A number of studies on parental choice have been carried out in inner London. One such early study which touched on primary school choice was that by Varlaam *et al* (1985). As part of a study on parents' attitudes towards primary schooling, a question was asked about the main reason for choosing the primary school their child was attending.

Again, proximity emerged as the most important factor with nearly half the parents reporting that the school was the nearest and with more in manual than non-manual occupations citing this reason. Just over one-fifth of the parents mentioned that the school had been recommended.

A recent study carried out in inner London (Royal Borough of Kensington and Chelsea, 1993), was concerned specifically with why parents choose schools in other local education authorities. The study involved questionnaires being sent to a sample of 1,655 parents resident in the borough who had opted to send their child to either primary or secondary schools outside the borough. Of the 437 completed returns, 58 were from the parents of primary-aged pupils. Again, the location of the school was given as a reason by the largest number of parents (41 per cent). The fact that the school was a religious school was mentioned by 36 per cent, the attitude of the school staff by 26 per cent and academic reasons by 19 per cent. It is also interesting to note that religious reasons were given by more parents of girls than boys, and by more speakers of English as a second language than those with English as a first language. Those with English as a first language tended to mention the quality of the school's staff more than did speakers of English as a second language.

Secondary school choice – parents of children already in secondary school

Many more studies examining choice of secondary school have been carried out. One of the earliest was carried out by Elliott (1982) who interviewed parents of children attending one secondary school; he found that, for some parents, proximity of the school to home was an important reason for choosing a particular school. He also found that children were given a major say in the choice of school. 'Our child wanted to go to the school' was found to be a 'very important' reason for 38 per cent of parents, while the most frequently given reason – cited as 'very important' by 50 per cent of parents – was 'provides a balanced all-round education'.

A large-scale study examining the general issue of parental choice was carried out by Stillman and Maychell (1986), in which parents' views were sought across four very different local education authorities (LEAs) as to their reasons for choosing a school. In all four authorities, the parents' most commonly mentioned important factor when choosing a school was its academic record (mentioned by 52 per cent). The second most frequently stated item was good discipline (38 per cent) and the third was close proximity (28 per cent).

Several studies have also been carried out in inner London. One early study carried out by West *et al* (1984) focused on parents' attitudes to school and as part of this examined reasons for choosing secondary schools. A total of 216 parents of first-year secondary school pupils were interviewed. A third of the parents mentioned that one reason for choosing the school their child was currently attending was that it was close to home; 31 per cent mentioned the school's good reputation and over a quarter (29 per cent) mentioned that relations went there. Other reasons included good discipline (23 per cent), the school being single-sex (20 per cent), recommendation (19 per cent) and the fact that the school was a church school (18 per cent). The school's 'good reputation' was given as the *most important reason* by the largest percentage of parents (20 per cent), followed by relations at the school (12 per cent) and proximity to home (10 per cent). Some interesting differences between parents from different ethnic groups and from different social classes emerged with more parents of Asian than English, Scottish, Welsh or Irish or Caribbean backgrounds selecting their child's school because it was single-sex. More working-class parents than middle-class parents also selected their child's school because it was single-sex.

A more recent study in inner London was carried out by Hunter (1991). This study was particularly concerned with the issue of single-sex and mixed schooling. It was found that the reasons spontaneously mentioned as being important when choosing a secondary school were good discipline (mentioned by 47 per cent), proximity of the school (42 per cent), good examination results (39 per cent) and the school's accessibility (34 per cent). Over a quarter of the parents (26 per cent) mentioned the fact that the school was single-sex. The reasons identified as 'most important' were good discipline (mentioned by 15 per cent), good examination results (15 per cent) and the school being single-sex or near to home (12 per cent each). Parents with children at voluntary (religious) schools were more likely to give weight to good discipline and to an emphasis on good examination results than those with children at county schools, while a majority of the latter group gave greatest priority to the proximity of the school to home. Parents from different ethnic groups also tended to have different priorities when choosing schools; those with African or Caribbean backgrounds most often gave the school's emphasis on good examination results as their main reason for choosing it, while Asian parents most often gave the school being single-sex as their main reason. Discipline appeared to be a priority for both skilled and semi-skilled or unskilled manual groups, while the school's emphasis on good examination results, together with the fact that the school was single-sex, were the most important for the largest proportion of non-manual working parents.

The study carried out recently in inner London by the Royal Borough of Kensington and Chelsea (see above), also examined parents' reasons for choosing their child's current (or preferred) school. A total of 370 questionnaires were analysed. Overall, 38 per cent of the parents gave academic reasons for choosing a school in another borough, such as the range of subjects, examination results, the quality of teaching, teachers' expectations or homework. Academic reasons were mentioned more often by girls' parents than by boys' parents. A quarter of parents were influenced either by recommendations from friends or relatives, or because they already knew someone or had an older child at the school and had a favourable opinion of the school. The importance of siblings and friends was greater for parents who chose county schools than religious schools and particularly important for Muslims and also those with no religion at county schools. Discipline was mentioned by 23 per cent of the parents and more parents selected Church of England and Roman Catholic schools for their discipline than those who chose county schools. Discipline was more important for the parents who selected boys' schools than girls' or mixed schools. Location was mentioned by 21 per cent of the parents and religion by 19 per cent. Sixteen per cent of parents mentioned single-sex education with girls' parents being more keen on this type of education than boys' parents. Muslim parents were the principal group to prefer single-sex education.

Choice of secondary school – parents of children in primary school

Although a number of studies have thus examined choice of secondary schools these have tended to focus on the parents of children who have already started secondary school. This method has the disadvantage of relying on parents' recollections of past events, and possible re-interpretations or post-hoc justifications of their reasons for choosing the school they did. Several studies, however, have been carried out with the parents of primary school children.

One of the earliest was carried out by Alston (1985), who explored the views of parents in inner London before their child's transfer to secondary school. The parents were asked about the factors that they regarded as important when selecting a secondary school; nearly two-thirds of the parents (65 per cent) said their child wanted to go there, 53 per cent said the school was close to home or easily accessible, 48 per cent mentioned that the school had 'many facilities' and the same number said that it had a good reputation for behaviour and discipline. The school's good organisation was mentioned by two-fifths of the parents and its reputation for good examination results by 38 per cent. Smaller numbers of parents had taken into account other factors – a quarter had opted consciously for a single-sex school and almost a fifth had shown a preference for a mixed school. Most parents had taken a number of different factors into account when choosing their child's secondary school; when asked to identify the factor that had been most important to them, the child's choice and the school's reputation for discipline were both mentioned by just under a fifth of the parents, with ease of access and good examination results being mentioned by around 10 per cent.

Adler *et al* (1989) also examined reasons for choosing a secondary school. Parents who had considered a school other than the catchment area school were asked what the four most important reasons were for wanting their child to attend the requested school. The most frequently occurring reasons for selecting the requested school were, first, the judgement that the child would be happiest at the chosen school and, second, the fact that the child said she or he would prefer to go there; there were some geographical variations, with better discipline being mentioned next most frequently in three of the four locations, and ease of access in the other.

More recently, West and Varlaam (1991) in a study carried out in inner London, found that the reasons mentioned spontaneously as being important when choosing a secondary school, were the child wanting to go (71 per cent), good discipline (67 per cent), good examination results (54 per cent) and ease of access (53 per cent). The 'most important' factors, however, were good discipline (28 per cent), the child wanting to go there (13 per cent), a good choice of subjects and the fact that the school was a church school (10 per cent each).

Once again the child wanting to go to the school, good discipline and ease of access emerged as key factors.

Coldron and Boulton (1991) gathered data from 222 families with children who were in the last year of primary school. Parents were asked to give their reasons for choosing the particular secondary school their child would be attending the next academic year. Thirty-two per cent mentioned the proximity of the school, 16 per cent indicated that a sibling attends or attended that school, 15 per cent that the child's friends were attending and 10 per cent that the school was the child's preference or the best for education. It was also found that the child's preference was more likely to be cited by those in skilled, semi-skilled, and unskilled manual occupations than by others, while the response 'best for education' was given by a much higher percentage of those in the professional and semi-professional categories.

A different approach was used by Bastow (1991a, b), who carried out a questionnaire study of 1,250 parents of children in their last three years of primary school in a large town outside London. Parents were asked to rank or rate sets of given characteristics of schools in order of importance for their child. They were also asked to list the five most important factors that influenced their choice. Parents were grouped according to their preferred secondary school, and it was found using multi-level modelling that they discriminated on the basis of whether schools were co-educational or single-sex (44 per cent of the discriminatory power), on the basis of whether they are denominational (10 per cent) and on whether the school was closest to the family home (5 per cent). A school's performance on examinations did not have sufficient discriminatory power to be included in the analysis, but it was found that when asked to say what they thought the five most important characteristics of a good school were, the most important were that the child would be happy (mentioned by 14 per cent), good overall examination results (10 per cent) and good discipline (8 per cent).

A recent study carried out by West and David (see West et al, 1993) also examined factors important in parents' choice of a secondary school for their child. The study involved interviewing 70 parents in two inner London boroughs about the process of choosing a secondary school for their child. Around a third of the parents spontaneously mentioned that good examination results were an important factor with a similar proportion mentioning the atmosphere or ethos of the school and just over quarter mentioning the proximity of the school to the child's home. The most important aspects, however, related to the school's academic record/good education (mentioned by 27 per cent of the parents) and the child's wishes/happiness (mentioned by 20 per cent of the parents). Some interesting differences between groups of parents emerged in the factors they considered to be important. As has been found in previous studies in inner London, there was a trend for more parents of girls than boys to report that the school being single-sex was important, and a trend for more white and Asian than black parents to mention that the ethos or atmosphere of the school was important; more white than black or Asian parents mentioned proximity to home as important. In addition, significantly more parents where the father or the mother were in a non-manual occupation indicated that the atmosphere or ethos was an important factor in their choice.

Ball *et al* (1993) have also examined choice of secondary school in the greater London area, but this time from a sociological perspective. They did not examine factors *per se*; however, they note in making choices there is a 'play off' between reputation and desirability on the one hand and factors such as distance and the match between the child and the school on the other. They also found that for working class parents the child's wishes are more often decisive while for middle class parents the child's input into the choice process is more limited. This supports the findings from other, more quantitative, research studies (West, 1993).

A further recent study by Webster *et al* (1993) examined choice of secondary school in the south-west of England. Parents of 68 children were asked among other things to comment on the single most important factor which influenced their choice of secondary school; siblings at the school was mentioned by 37 per cent of the parents, and proximity to home, academic achievements and facilities and atmosphere of the school by 16 per cent each.

Parents' choice of private schools

Comparatively little research has been carried out on parents' reasons for choosing private as opposed to state education for their children (see Walford, 1990).

The most detailed study of private education was carried out by Fox (1985). She interviewed the parents of 190 boys (boarders and day boys) in traditional public schools. She examined why parents chose public schools for their sons and found that one-third of the sample had a fundamental commitment to the private sector. Two-thirds of the sample gave clear reasons for their choice: 28 per cent had reasons classifiable as 'getting on better in life', 23 per cent believed that such schools would provide academic advantage, and a further 14 per cent were concerned that the schools should 'develop character and foster discipline'.

Johnson (1987) also examined the reasons parents give for using the private sector. Her research methods were less rigorous than those of Fox; 25 families who had responded to advertisements in the local press were interviewed. There are methodological problems with Johnson's work (see Walford, 1990, for a full discussion), but the range of reasons given for transfer from the state to private sector are interesting – the decline in the number of grammar schools and the demise of direct grant schools were specifically cited, with the associated idea that comprehensive schools did not offer an adequate education for children of high academic ability.

A questionnaire survey by MORI (1989) for the Independent Schools Information Service (ISIS) specifically examined parents' reasons for choosing the private (independent) system rather than the state system. A postal survey of 1,135 parents with children in their first year of preparatory school or first year of senior school was carried out and it was found that a higher standard of education was the reason most frequently given by parents for choosing the private system rather than the state system. Parents were asked about factors important in their choice of their child's current school; good discipline was mentioned by 86 per cent of the sample and examination results of the school by 79 per cent. The single most important factor, however, was the ability of the school to meet the child's individual needs (mentioned by 29 per cent), followed by examination results (14 per cent) and the school's reputation (10 per cent).

West (1992a,b) also carried out a small-scale study of 27 parents in an inner London borough to try and establish why parents who had used the state primary sector for their children's education were considering private secondary schooling for their children. This study found that over one-fifth of the sample were considering such a school because of the high academic ability of their child. When asked about factors important in their choice of a private senior school or state secondary school for their child, nearly half the parents spontaneously mentioned good discipline and a school that suited their child's needs; good examination results were mentioned by nearly half of the parents. The most important factor, however, for 22 per cent of the parents was the quality of the education (academic excellence) and for 19 per cent it was that it should suit the child's needs/desires.

Although they did not focus on choosing schools, Edwards *et al* (1989) asked parents with children at different types of schools in the private and public sectors – fee-payers and assisted places in the private sector and comprehensive and grammar in the state sector – which factors were 'very important' in their choice of secondary school. Overall, school ethos, examination results and access to higher education occurred most frequently. However, relatively more weight was given to the child's friends going to the school in the comprehensive sample than in the other groups of parents.

Pupils' Involvement in Choice of Secondary School

Until recently, relatively little research has focused on pupils' involvement in the choice process in relation to secondary schooling. However, in a number of studies pupils have been shown to have an important role to play in the decision-making process.

One of the earliest studies to have focused on pupils' views was carried out by Alston *et al* (1985). When asked who had decided which secondary school they should choose, nearly a quarter of the Year 6 (aged 10 to 11) sample said that their parents had made the choice, but a fifth said that they had made the decision themselves. However, the largest group (45 per cent) stated that the decision was a joint one, made by parents and pupils. A marked difference between the sexes was identified with almost twice as many boys as girls claiming to have made the decision themselves.

More recently, Thomas and Dennison (1991) carried out a questionnaire study with 72 pupils in their final year of primary education in an inner-city junior school in northern England. It was found that most pupils (60 per cent) reported that they made the decision about secondary school. Few (one in seven) claimed to have had no say in the final decision.

Walford (1991) also examined pupils' involvement in the choice process in the interviews and questionnaires carried out with pupils in their first and second years at Kingshurst City Technology College (CTC). Interviews with 45 second-year pupils (Year 8) took place and in these the process by which the decision to attend the CTC was made was explored. Pupils were asked explicitly if the choice had been their own choice or that of their parents. Nearly half said that it had been they who had made the final choice. About 40 per cent stated that they had made the decision together with their parents and about 10 per cent stated that the decision to apply to the CTC had been more influenced by their parents' views than their own.

A further study involving 399 pupils was carried out in an outer London LEA (West, Varlaam and Scott, 1991). Two-thirds of the pupils reported that both they and their parents (or adults with whom they lived) chose the school, with just under a fifth saying that they had made the choice and a similar proportion saying that their parents had made the choice. Interestingly, more Asian than European or African/Afro-Caribbean pupils reported that their parents had chosen their prospective high school. More European and African/Afro-Caribbean than Asian pupils said that they had chosen their prospective high school.

Two other recent studies have asked parents who chose their child's school. West *et al* (1993), for example, asked the parents in their study who had had the main responsibility for deciding the school for their child. Around three-quarters of the respondents reported that parents (generally the mother) had had the main responsibility; fewer than 10 per cent reported that their child had the main responsibility, while around one-sixth reported that the child and the parent(s) had the main responsibility.

However, the research carried out in the Royal Borough of Kensington and Chelsea (1993) with parents of children currently in secondary school found a much higher proportion of parents reporting that their child chose the school – about half of the parents reported that they had chosen their child's school alone, about a quarter chose with their child and a fifth allowed their child to choose.

Taken together, these studies suggest that parents and pupils differ about who actually makes the decision about the child's secondary school. Nevertheless, there is no doubt that the child plays an important part in the process of choosing a secondary school, although perhaps less so in middle-class families with children who are perceived to be particularly able (see West, 1993) than in other families.

Conclusions

The research reviewed indicates that parents take a number of factors into account when choosing a secondary school for their child.

At the primary stage, there is a general consensus that the school's location is of prime importance. At the secondary stage there is less consensus, with considerable variation between different studies in the proportions of respondents who cited particular reasons as important. This is not surprising as the studies differed considerably in both their approach and methods. In some studies, for example, lists of reasons for the respondents to choose from were used, while in others mostly open-ended questioning was used. Such variations in approach can easily lead to seemingly different results – for example, what appears as 'good reputation' in one study may easily be the same as another's 'good academic record'. In addition, the samples have frequently differed – some have comprised parents who are more highly educated and/or from more middle class backgrounds, some have consisted of parents in city areas, while others have consisted of parents in more rural areas; and some have considered the choice process retrospectively, while others have considered it at the time the choice is being made or even earlier (Bastow, 1991a,b). All of these factors are likely to have an impact on the results obtained. For example, the parents in the study carried out by Bastow may or may not have been seriously considering secondary schools at the time the survey was carried out (see West *et al*, 1993).

Nevertheless, certain factors do emerge as important in the studies reviewed. In many studies, proximity of the school or its location and performance issues (examination results or academic record) emerge. Good discipline is another factor that frequently emerges. Although a number of studies carried out with parents of children in Year 6 (fourth-year junior school) point to the 'child wanting to go' as an important factor, this is not a universal finding, and may be related to class differences and variations in the sample composition.

Temporal differences may also help to account for some of the differences found in relation to this factor. It is possible that parents are now focusing more on performance issues – school examination results – and performance-related issues – a pleasant atmosphere or ethos – than they were in the past.

The recent research by West *et al* (1993) was carried out before the first 'league tables' of examination results were published (in 1992), but at a time when examination results for individual schools were nevertheless widely available. The most frequently mentioned 'most important' factors to emerge in this study were the school's academic record/good education; this contrasts with a number of earlier studies in which 'good discipline' emerges as one of the 'most important' factors.

Apart from methodological differences, variations in the findings are also likely to reflect differences in the range and type of schools available in the areas where the various studies took place – for example, in an area with only one or two mixed schools, fewer parents are likely to consider choosing a mixed school for their child. However, the findings from a number of studies do indicate that for a substantial minority of parents, the fact that a school is either single-sex or mixed or a religious school is an important factor.

It is postulated that parents from different ethnic, social and religious groups choose or opt for secondary schools using different criteria. For a number of parents, basic 'structural' criteria have to be fulfilled in relation to school choice. Some parents, predominantly middle class, will only consider independent schooling. For some Asian and Muslim parents, and those with strong views about the importance of girls being educated away from the distractions of boys, the fact that the school is single-sex appears to be of paramount importance. For some parents of boys, the fact that a school is mixed is of paramount importance. For some Christian parents (and indeed some Jewish and some Muslim parents) the fact that the school is religious is of paramount importance, and for some non-religious parents such a school is also of paramount importance perhaps because such schools are perceived to be well disciplined.

Another structural criterion is the proximity of the school. For some parents the choice process is not 'active' but 'passive' – such parents may or may not leave the 'choice' of secondary school to their child; however, there is an assumption that because it is nearby and local children attend that school, there is no real 'decision' to make. In a similar way, families who live in rural areas will have a restricted 'choice' as few schools will be easily accessible for the majority of children.

Not all parents will need such structural criteria to be fulfilled. Some parents may be more concerned with 'dynamic' factors; they may for example, opt for the school their child wants to go to or where the child's friends are going. Others may want a school at which their child will receive what is perceived to be a high-quality education; such a school may or may not be in the independent sector, it may or may not be single-sex or religious and may or may not be in close proximity to home. Rather it will be a school that is perceived to have 'good' examination results and stretches children academically; the overriding factors in such cases are performance or performance-related factors.

At the primary stage, then, there is a high degree of consensus, at least among parents who use the state sector, about factors important in the choice of a primary school. At the secondary stage, there is a degree of consensus, at least in general terms, but this conceals some marked and interesting differences between parents with different social, ethnic and religious backgrounds. The use of the concepts of 'structural' and 'dynamic' factors might be one way of trying to understand further and predict how the choice process works in individual cases.

Acknowledgements

I would like to thank Robert West and Hazel Pennell for helpful comments on an earlier draft of this chapter.

References

Adler, M, Petch, A and Tweedie, J (1989) *Parental Choice and Educational Policy* Edinburgh, Edinburgh University Press.

Alston, C (1985) *Secondary Transfer Project, Bulletin 3: The Views of Parents before Transfer* (RS 991/85), London, ILEA.

Alston, C, Sammons, P and Mortimore, P (1985) *Secondary Transfer Project, Bulletin 2: The Views of Primary School Pupils* (RS 990/85), London, ILEA.

Ball, S J, Bowe, R and Gewirtz, S (1993) 'Circuits of schooling: a sociological exploration of parental choice in social class contexts' *Sociological Review*, 41, 3.

Ballion, R and Oeuvrard, F (1991) 'Le choix de l'etablissement scolaire: le cas des lycees parisiens' *Education et Formation*, 29, pp 27–41.

Bastow, B (1991a) *A Study of Factors Affecting Parental Choice of Secondary School*, PhD thesis, Institute of Education, University of London.

Bastow, B (1991b) 'How to single out a school' *Times Educational Supplement*, 2 August.

Coldron, J and Boulton, P (1991) 'Happiness as a criterion of parents' choice of school' *Journal of Education Policy*, 6, 2, pp 169–78.

David, M E (1993) *Parents, Gender and Education Reform* Cambridge, Polity Press.

Edwards, T, Fitz, J and Whitty, G (1989) *The State and Private Education: An Evaluation of the Assisted Places Scheme* London, Falmer Press.

Elliott, J (1982) 'How do parents choose and judge secondary schools?' in McCormick, R (ed) *Calling Education to Account* London, Open University Press.

Fox, I (1985) *Private Schools and Public Issues: The Parents' View* Basingstoke, Macmillan.

Hughes, M, Wikeley, F and Nash, T (1990) *Parents and the National Curriculum: An Interim Report* School of Education, University of Exeter.

Hunter, J (1991) 'Parental choice of secondary school' *Educational Research*, 33, 1, pp 31–41.

Johnson, D (1987) *Private Schools and State Schools: Two Systems or One?* Milton Keynes, Open University Press.

Royal Borough of Kensington and Chelsea (1993) *Selecting a School: A Survey of Parents*, Education Research Paper 1/93.

MORI (1989) *How and Why Parents Choose an Independent School* London, MORI.

Stillman, A and Maychell, K (1986) *Choosing Schools: Parents, LEAs and the 1980 Education Act* Windsor, NFER–Nelson.

Thomas, A and Dennison, B (1991) 'Parental or pupil choice – who really decides in urban schools?' *Educational Management and Administration*, 19, 4, pp 243–49.

Varlaam, A, Woods, J, Mortimore, P, and Sammons, P (1985) *Parents and Primary Schools* (RS 987/85) London, ILEA.

Walford, G (1990) *Privatization and Privilege in Education* London, Routledge.

Walford, G (1991) 'Choice of school at the first City Technology College', *Educational Studies*, 17, 1, pp 65–75.

Webster, A, Owen, G and Crome, D (1993) *School Marketing: Making it Easy for Parents to Select your School* Bristol, Avec Designs.

West, A (1992a) *Choosing Schools: Why do Parents Opt for Private Schools or Schools in Other LEAs?* (commissioned by Islington Education Department), Clare Market Paper 1, Centre for Educational Research, London School of Economics and Political Science.

West, A (1992b) 'Factors affecting choice of school for middle class parents: implications for marketing' *Educational Management and Administration*, 20, 4, pp 212–21.

West, A (1993) 'Choosing schools: are different factors important for different parents?' in Smith, M and Busher, H (eds) *Managing Schools in an*

Uncertain Environment: Resources, Marketing and Power Sheffield, Sheffield Hallam University for BEMAS (British Educational Management and Administration Society).

West, A, David, M, Hailes, J, Ribbens, J and Hind, A (1993) *Choosing a Secondary School: The Parents' and Pupils' Stories* Clare Market Paper 7, Centre for Educational Research, London School of Economics and Political Science.

West, A and Varlaam, A (1991) 'Choice of secondary school: parents of junior school children' *Educational Research*, 33, 1, pp 22–30.

West, A, Varlaam, A and Mortimore, P (1984) 'Attitudes to school: a study of the parents of first year pupils' in Hargreaves, D (ed) *Improving Secondary Schools, Research Studies* London, ILEA.

West, A, Varlaam, A and Scott, G (1991) 'Choice of high schools: pupils' perceptions' *Educational Research*, 33, 3, pp 205–15.

Chapter 9

School Responses to the Quasi-market

Philip Woods

In a market, producers are supposed to respond to consumer choice. The consumer (in theory) is sovereign. But consumers can only enjoy 'monarchical' rights if producers are able and willing to provide the goods or services they want. Hence, the rationale behind the education reforms aimed at enhancing parental choice is that – coupled with pupil-led funding and local management of schools – *choice will change schools*. It will, it is claimed, alter for the better how schools operate and the kind of service they give. According to the government:

> Limited opportunities and limited choice have been replaced by greater choice and greater access ... More diversity allows schools to respond more effectively to the needs of the local and national community. The greater their autonomy, the greater the responsiveness of schools. Parents know best the needs of their children ... Children themselves, as they grow older and mature, often have a well developed sense of their needs and a good grasp of the quality of the teaching they receive. (Department for Education/Welsh Office, 1992, pp 1–2)

Patterns of schools 'that reflect the priorities of local authority planners, should be complemented or replaced by schools that reflect more widely the wishes and aspirations of parents' (ibid, p 43). Is this happening? This chapter outlines some of the ways by which schools are adapting and responding to the market-like environment (or quasi-market) in which they now exist. It draws on data and experience gained from the Parental and School Choice Interaction (PASCI) study, a project begun in 1990 with funding from the Economic and Social Research Council (ESRC) and set to continue until the end of 1995 (see

Figure 9.1: *Typology of school responses*

Response	Purpose and scope
Competitive within this three main types of activity can be distinguished:	To increase or maintain the number of pupils at the school
• **substantive change**	• includes changes in the school's central educational activities (such as curriculum and teaching methods) and the way it organises itself; also includes changes in intake selection and character of school
• **environmental 'scanning and interpretation'** (*environmental scanning*)	• concerned with how a school perceives its 'market', finding out what influences parents' school preferences
• **promotional activity**	• action intended to raise the school's profile, improve its image
Income-enhancing	To secure income over and above the school budget based on formula-funding, through fund-raising, sponsorship deals, and so on
Efficiency-increasing	To get the most of the school budget and concentrate resources on the school's central educational activities
Political	To influence politicians and/or officials and encourage them to make changes (such as in the funding formula) which will benefit the school
Collaborative	To obtain benefits from working in co-operation with other schools: co-operation can be concerned with achieving any of the above aims; includes co-operative action aimed at eliminating or reducing competition

Centre for Educational Policy and Management, 1993). This includes a databank of school responses to choice and competition which draws on examples of responsiveness reported in printed media and on information gathered through contacts and opportunistic samples. Its aim is to capture the range of what schools are doing. It has enabled the development of a typology of school responses which is being refined as the main phase of the PASCI study proceeds (Woods, 1992).

How Schools are Responding

The typology outlined in Figure 9.1 is an abstracted representation of the main ways in which schools appear to be responding. It is intended as an overview and guide to further investigations (rather than implying a false rigidity or simplicity in school responsiveness). It attempts to classify responses by schools, not schools themselves. Schools may undertake actions that fall into one or several of these categories. In particular, a school may be competitive in some of its activities while collaborating in others. Different responses may also interact. Thus, for example, what is discovered about parental preferences through *environmental scanning* may lead to *substantive changes* aimed at making the school more attractive. The discussion below focuses mainly on *competitive* and *collaborative* responses as it is within the areas represented by these categories that schools appear to be most active.

Competitive responses

Increased emphasis on promoting, or selling, the school is widespread. It has led to a burgeoning literature on promotional and marketing techniques (Glatter, Johnson and Woods, 1993). The kinds of initiatives being undertaken by schools include: closer links with 'feeder' schools (this perhaps being the most popular means of promoting the school), production of more attractive brochures and other means (such as videos) of presenting what the school offers, efforts to gain enhanced press coverage, increasing opportunities for prospective parents to visit the school and improving the school's appearance, as well as other external facets of image such as school uniform (Woods, 1992, 1993b).

Of particular interest are *substantive changes* which schools make. It is upon these changes that the success of the reforms (in the terms outlined in the introduction) must hinge: the extent and nature of these will determine how far the quasi-market leads to improved educational standards and to schools which increasingly reflect the 'wishes and aspirations of parents'.

With this in mind, it is pertinent to note that marketing is not (or should not be) only about selling. It is about being responsive to consumers. Put succinctly, it is about finding out what consumers want and giving it to them (Glatter, Johnson and Woods, 1993). If parents are concerned about what goes on within the school and the quality of learning it provides (ie its central educational activities), then marketing by schools should also be about that (assuming that school decision-makers want to meet parental wishes and that parents have some means of assessing what happens within the school). As one headteacher put it (whose school had tried the 'glossy brochure' approach and moved on from this), 'marketing is what goes on in this building'.

The incidence of *substantive change* is particularly difficult to assess. There are many factors influencing schools (not least the introduction and reappraisals of the National Curriculum). It is a challenging research task to identify the extent to which the need to compete for parental choices has brought about or had a significant bearing upon changes in a school's organisation, policies and practices. Evidence suggests that the perceived competitive position of schools and enhanced emphasis on parental choice are factors (acting together with other influences) in bringing about *substantive changes* in some schools (Woods, 1992, 1993b). Schools with sixth-forms, for example, have increased the range of courses available to students (introducing BTEC courses) as a means of making what they have to offer as a school more attractive. The impact to date of choice and competition on the school curriculum generally is scant, however. Many school decision-makers feel constrained by the National Curriculum (even so, it may be that in certain areas, such as foreign languages, schools will be keen to offer more options where feasible). Other examples of policy changes in secondary schools include requiring pupils in the lower years to undertake formal examinations, the introduction of set homework nights, reinforcement of the school as a caring institution, and greater willingness to use fixed-term exclusions as a means of discipline (see below). Concern about the 'signals' schools convey can extend to areas that are not directly educational (though they are part of curricular experience in the wider sense): thus the headteacher and governors at one school decided to negotiate with the LEA school-meals service for a higher standard that would impress parents.

It cannot be claimed that such actions result uniquely from the competitive forces of the quasi-market. What our data show is evidence that school decision-makers' views of parental preferences have been influential in encouraging changes of this sort in certain schools. It also has to be emphasised that such changes appear to have occurred in a small number of schools (and not all of them have been introduced by any one school), and that the more detailed data being generated by the PASCI study relate to secondary schools. Hard evidence on how many schools throughout the country are making *substantive changes* (and the preponderance of different types of such change) is not available. Monitoring of the unfolding impact of competitive forces is needed over a number of years.

An example of systematic *environmental scanning*, followed by *substantive change*, is offered by one secondary school in London. This school carried out a SWOT (Strengths, Weaknesses, Opportunities and Threats) analysis (Weeks, 1992). The purpose of the exercise was to establish the reasoning behind parental choice of secondary school, to identify the school's strengths and weaknesses in comparison with its competitors, and to enable development of a strategy aimed at attracting more pupils. The analysis involved a number of stages, including a survey of parents of Year 7 pupils, and resulted in changes intended to enhance the school's attractiveness. These included provision of a better range of courses at sixth-form level and improvements to the school grounds and buildings, these latter improvements being overseen by a committee of the school's pupils.

It would seem that generally, however, schools are more enthusiastic about 'selling' themselves (*promotional activity*) than finding out what parents and others think about the school (*environmental scanning*) (Woods, 1992). There are indications nevertheless that some schools may be developing more systematic ways of obtaining feedback from parents (Woods, 1993b). Research in the USA on the impact of parental choice suggests that smaller schools with a specific focus (private Catholic schools or public schools emphasising a curricular theme) tend to be more responsive to parents. The researchers make the point that such 'structural responsiveness has more to do with deliberative planning or strategising how a school might interact more effectively with parents, rather than leaving such interactions to chance' (Goldring and Bauch, 1993, p 25). 'Structural responsiveness' can take many forms. Initiatives along these lines – including surveys of parents, availability of parent governors for informal discussion at school events, and one-to-one discussions between senior staff and all pupils in their final year to obtain their views of the school – have been prompted to some extent in some schools by greater competition (Woods, 1993b).

A further aspect of *substantive change* is the option for a school to restrict or alter its intake by means of changes to admissions criteria and, in its most extreme case, to change the character of the school (by, for example, becoming a selective grammar). At the time of writing one school (in Cumbria) has been granted permission to alter its comprehensive status and to become a grammar school, whilst two Hertfordshire schools are to select 50 per cent of their intake on the basis of tests. Some research suggests that a substantial number of grant-maintained schools discriminate among applicants on the basis (in part) of interviews, reports and examinations. In the more competitive climate characterised by examination and test results 'the pressure to control intakes has proved irresistible for some schools ... [though] ... there is nothing inherent in opting out that compels a school to become selective' (Bush *et al*, 1993, pp 95, 106). At the same time, a majority of LEAs appear to be broadly content with the operation of grant-maintained admissions (Morris, 1993). Selection of up to 10 per cent of pupils 'on the basis of ability or aptitude in one or more of music, art, drama and physical education' can be undertaken without its being deemed a change in the character, and hence without the school requiring permission to do so (Department for Education, 1992, p 14). A recent survey of LEAs suggested that, where an LEA felt there were problems (in relation to LEA-controlled or grant-maintained schools), they centred on the unclear purpose of schools' interviews of parents and/or prospective pupils and on signs of resistance to accept youngsters perceived as future problems for the school (Morris, 1993). Another study, investigating the impact of local management of schools on all schools in one LEA, failed to find evidence of 'cream skimming' of the more able pupils (Levacic, 1993). The long-term effect of competitive pressures may lead more schools in the direction of selection, but at present it is difficult to assess how far this will spread among schools.

The issue of selection relates to that of specialisation. A more market-like environment is supposed to encourage diversity of provision to cater for differing interests and aptitudes. It is not clear, however, that competitive forces to date have been the main force behind moves to specialise. Government initiatives appear to be of greater significance, whether at local government level (for example, Wandsworth's 'magnet schools' – see Bush *et al*, 1993, p 99) or centrally (as with the development of City Technology Schools and a network of technology colleges – see Department for Education/Welsh Office, 1992). Nonetheless, we may see in the future local competitive forces in some areas encouraging schools to specialise or encouraging the formation of new state schools to meet particularly strong parental demands (such as that for Muslim education).

Besides selection, another means of controlling a school's pupil population is exclusion of those who are especially troublesome and/or least likely to contribute to the academic performance of the school. In a competitive environment there can be several incentives to use pupil exclusion. For example, dealing sharply with behaviour problems can send a 'signal' to parents and the local community that the school is serious about maintaining good discipline; permanent exclusion of pupils likely to perform badly in tests and public examinations will help improve the school's position in the local league table; removing disruptive pupils from the school might allow other pupils to get on with their work and progress more quickly. Figures suggest that permanent exclusions have increased in recent years (Department for Education, 1993). This may partly be the result of such incentives, though there is no evidence to conclude that it is mainly or wholly a consequence of the quasi-market. Competitive pressures may act sometimes in the opposite direction, on the grounds that a high number of exclusions may suggest to some parents that a school has problems and is best avoided. There may be greater flexibility when it comes to fixed-term exclusions. One secondary school, struggling with a poor reputation and located in a deprived area, saw short, fixed-term exclusions as a way of signalling its intention of dealing seriously with troublemakers and as one means of helping to improve its reputation.

Income-enhancing, efficiency-increasing and political responses

Other responses in the typology – *income-enhancing, efficiency-increasing* and *political* – are distinguishable from *competitive* responses and constitute discrete categories. They represent different ways of dealing with the consequences of a market-like environment in which funding is determined largely by formulae based on pupil numbers. Both *income-enhancing* and *efficiency-increasing* are ways by which a school can increase its capacity to carry out its educational activities. *Income-enhancing* is a means by which, instead of or in addition to attracting more pupils, a school can gain more resources. We are seeing numbers of schools becoming more enterprising in their methods. These include employment of full-time marketing managers charged with a duty to enhance school income and (in one instance) establishing the school as a trading company. With regard to *efficiency-increasing,* from the data we have it appears that schools are tending to pursue this via collaborative efforts with other schools aimed at reaping the benefits of economies of scale.

Political responses to the new environment created by the reforms appear to be concerned with the impact of formula funding on school budgets. This is of particular concern to many small primary schools. In a market the classic response to inadequate revenue is to increase custom – in the case of schools, pupils. This is not necessarily a feasible option for small schools in, say, a rural area in which the number of available pupils is limited. One response therefore – instead of a competitive one – is to seek to alter the groundrules that determine how monies are distributed between schools. Such *political* responses are not confined to rural areas, however. For example, a small first school in Bradford responded to its budget reduction, following the introduction of local management of schools, by organising a parents' action group to campaign on its behalf. Political lobbying by businesses in private competitive markets is not unusual. Private businesses are not driven by economic theory, but by their assessment of what the best strategy is to enable them to survive and prosper. Such assessments sometimes impel business people to seek changes in the law or provision of state subsidies. This kind of response to the challenges of the education quasi-market is equally open to schools where school decision-makers consider it may reap benefits.

Collaborative responses

Collaborative responses, involving schools working together, is a significant trend in response to the competitive forces of the education quasi-market. The incentives to financial collaboration, and some of the forms this takes, have been outlined by Levacic and Woods (1994). Benefits of such collaboration include economies of scale, the sharing of 'goods' such as information or joint marketing, risk pooling (for example, arranging joint cover for staff absences), and avoidance of the costs of wasteful competition. The forms this cooperation takes vary from formally organised partnerships which cover a range of activities and schools, to more narrowly conceived, less formal arrangements whereby agreement is reached on a single resource-sharing activity (such as shared use of a group of secondary schools' sixth-forms).

Examples of the former include Community Links Across Sandhurst Primaries (CLASP) and the South Bristol Federation. CLASP is a consortium of six primary schools in Sandhurst which are working together in order to promote primary education 'as a keystone in the development of children's education', to establish partnerships with businesses and the local community and to eliminate wasteful duplications of effort involved in maintaining business contacts as individual schools. It has a formal constitution 'to protect the individual character of each of the schools, and to ensure that any actions taken by the group were agreed unanimously by all six heads', and has negotiated deals with major companies, such as Rank Xerox, for resources to contribute to children's learning opportunities (Mesley, 1991).

The South Bristol Federation consists of six comprehensive schools, over 20 primary schools and South Bristol College, and has a full-time Director paid for from the budgets of the member institutions. Its purpose is to share resources and expertise, communicate information for the benefit of all, provide opportunities for the development of materials for use in its schools, promote a greater awareness and understanding of different phases of education for the benefit of 'all our children, students and staff', facilitate strategies for financial benefit, and to provide a collective voice for responding to local and national educational issues and 'securing resource entitlements' (South Bristol Federation, 1992). The Federation is active, for example, in providing joint in-service training, facilitating cross-phase collaboration, and providing enhanced curricular opportunities such as 'Excellence in Sports' days which give pupils the chance to be coached by top players in different sports. The philosophy underlying the Federation places emphasis on serving the community (while respecting parents' rights to school choice) rather than on schools competing. It is expressed in this way by the headteacher of one of the member primary schools:

> The Federation counters the divisiveness between schools by providing an equal amount of support for all schools, by allowing schools to feel part of a bigger whole, by very much stressing unity and collaboration and by bringing about benefits to all schools within the Federation, benefits that perhaps are greater than those that we would otherwise gain from working on our own.

These examples illustrate the extent and formality of partnerships between schools that are growing up in some parts of the country. Some are expressly concerned to avoid competitiveness among local schools (as with the South Bristol Federation). It should be emphasised that there is a range of types of collaborative relationship beyond such formal partnerships or federations. *Collaborative* initiatives may be aimed at just one activity, such as joint marketing, cooperation in implementation of the National Curriculum, sharing of a bursar, or joint political lobbying. Thus *collaborative* responses can be aimed at any of the other categories in the typology. They can be aimed at making a group of schools more competitive, raising additional funds, increasing efficiency, or lending schools greater weight in contacts with political decision-makers. Whatever their goal, it is clear that the quasi-market in schooling is not necessarily antithetical to cooperative strategies.

Concluding Remarks

As observed at the outset of this chapter, the 'market hypothesis' is that *choice will change schools* and that patterns of schools will reflect more widely the wishes and aspirations of parents. It is not possible here to provide a definitive answer on the extent to which this hypothesis will be confirmed or otherwise as the quasi-market develops. A number of observations can be made, however.

Limitations, unevenness and multiformity

The quasi-market does appear to be acting as a lever of change in some places. We have noted that there are examples of schools responding by making *substantive changes* and adopting more structured ways of *environmental scanning*. However, responses are limited and patchy. There is no evidence at present of major or sweeping changes in schools' central educational areas as a result of attention to parents' preferences. Indeed, it would appear that schools tend to be more willing to engage in promoting themselves than in establishing systematic means of being responsive to parents. Yet without the latter, the aim of providing a pattern of service in line with what parents want is unlikely to be achieved.

Where schools are responding, they are not reacting in a uniformly competitive way. It is more appropriate to think in terms of a continuum, stretching from the 'stand-alone', aggressively competing school on the one hand, to the partnership-seeking school which tries to eliminate competition and replace it with a community of cooperating institutions on the other. In practice schools tend to be found along the gradations between these two positions.

In many areas the scope for exercising choice (and hence for competition to operate) is very limited. School responsiveness depends on a number of factors: the competitive context of the school (ie its local competitive arena; see Glatter and Woods, 1993), the views of school decision-makers, the school's tradition and ethos, and its ability to attract pupils without making educational changes (thus a popular school with a high reputation may be engaged in strategies to keep parents at a distance or to select 'desirable' pupils). Undersubscribed schools have a greater incentive to be responsive, but may concentrate on making themselves attractive to certain (notably middle class) parents (ibid) and/or find themselves constrained in their capacity to act by a budget linked to pupil numbers. As a consequence, there are built-in dangers of inequalities resulting from the quasi-market and no assurance that it will automatically increase choice and educational opportunities for all. Indeed, if policies such as pupil selection and exclusion were to be used increasingly by schools in response to competitive forces, the effect would be to decrease choice and opportunity for many. Such policies need to be monitored very closely, most particularly at local level because of the local nature of schooling quasi-markets.

Levers of change

Reliance only or primarily on choice as a means of making schools more responsive is unlikely to succeed. In the rhetoric which underpins pro-market policies, much faith is placed in market forces as an effective lever of change. But it is clear from the above that competitive forces act neither automatically nor evenly across the system. Over the last two decades or so the climate for parental involvement has steadily become more favourable and many practical initiatives have been undertaken. Much of this development has depended on 'persuasion' as a lever of change, for example, by argument, by demonstrating through research the importance of the home in educational progress, and developing and publicising practical parental involvement schemes (see, for example, Macbeth, 1989; Bastiani and Bailey, 1992; Jones et al, 1992; Merttens and Vass, 1993). Initiatives in parental involvement have tended to concentrate on matters such as information for parents and home-reading schemes, rather than facilitating parental influence in school decision-making, though there are examples of the latter and indications that choice and competition may encourage schools to experiment in this (Woods, 1993b). Nonetheless, the role of 'persuasion' is critical, providing the 'professional capital' from which school decision-makers can draw, as manifested, for example, in the set of materials based on detailed research and development work in Scotland aimed at enabling a school to evaluate itself and be responsive to pupils, parents and teachers (HM Inspector of Schools, 1992). Effective ways of putting responsiveness into operation are essential, and these do not arise automatically through the exercise of parental choice. Levers of change in addition to that of competitive forces are needed.

Towards a broad notion of responsiveness

The strength of *collaborative* responses, although not the avowed intention behind the reforms, should perhaps have been expected. Forms of cooperation are not unusual within the private sector (Thompson *et al*, 1991). Moreover, there is no one model of the market into which, *a priori*, schooling fits or must remain. Indeed, if the model underlying the reforms was that of schools as small or medium-size businesses operating in a private, competitive market (Glatter and Woods, 1992) – a model derived from the Thatcher years – the realities are significantly different. Hence, this chapter refers to the quasi-market in which schools now operate. Another perspective is to see state schooling as an 'internal market' which is highly regulated and not profit-driven and which differs markedly from a private 'external market' (Levacic, 1992).

As Ball observes, markets are 'neither natural nor neutral phenomena, they are socially and politically constructed' (Ball, 1993, p 8). One of the key elements shaping a quasi-market is the scope and nature of central state controls. The statutory national curriculum exemplifies this. Indeed, it has been observed that in comparison with other reformed public services, 'schooling is unique in the extent to which quasi-markets have been accompanied by an extension of central hierarchical control which specifies the product on behalf of the customer' (Levacic, 1993). Commentators on the 1992 Education Bill (proceeding through Parliament at the time of writing) reinforce the point, noting that it 'undeniably represents a further strengthening of the powers of central government' (Morris and Fowler, 1993, p 2).

Thus the impact of the quasi-market, and the ways in which schools respond to it, need to be understood in part by reference to the macro-environment. This provides the political and administrative context for the local competitive arenas in which school decision-makers and parents make their decisions (Glatter and Woods, 1993). Political decisions on matters such as formula funding, the National Curriculum, requirements to publish certain information, and so on are important factors in shaping the quasi-market. In consequence, the relationship of parents to schools cannot be confined to that of a 'narrow consumer', doing little more than choosing among competing schools (Woods, 1993a).

In evaluating the impact of the schooling quasi-market in terms of its responsiveness to the wishes of those it serves, a wider perspective is needed than that implied by parents as choice-makers. A broad notion of responsiveness is required, consistent with the nature of the relationship between parents and schools and the dependency of quasi-markets on the contextualising macro-environment. Elsewhere I have put forward the concept of the consumer-citizen as a more satisfactory conceptualisation of parents (and indeed pupils and other non-professionals) in relation to the schooling system, incorporating intrinsic aspects of that relationship which complement choice – in particular their active and creative roles and membership of a political community (Woods, 1993a). In a quasi-market, school responsiveness cannot be a function of individual choices alone. It is a matter determined at least as much by political decisions. If the system is to be shaped markedly by the needs and preferences of the consumer-citizen, then a strategy is required that incorporates more than one lever of change and which explicitly recognises the elemental importance of consumer-citizen participation at all levels of decision-making.

References

Ball S J (1993) 'Education markets, choice and social class: the market as a class strategy in the UK and USA' *British Journal of Sociology of Education*, 14, 1, pp 3–19.

Bastiani J and Bailey G (1992) *Directory of Home–School Initiatives in the UK* London, RSA.

Bush T, Coleman M and Glover D (1993) *Managing Autonomous Schools: The Grant-Maintained Experience* London, Paul Chapman.

Centre for Educational Policy and Management (1993) *Briefing Paper on the Main Phase of the PASCI Study* Milton Keynes, CEPAM, Open University School of Education.

Department for Education (1992) *Draft Circular on Admission Arrangements* London, DfE.

Department for Education (1993) 'A New Deal for "Out of School" Pupils' press release 126/93, April, London, DfE.

Department for Education/Welsh Office (1992) *Choice and Diversity: A new framework for schools* London, HMSO.

Glatter R and Woods P A (1992) *Parental Choice and School Decision-Making: Operating in a Market-Like Environment* Paper presented to 7th Regional Conference of the Commonwealth Council for Educational Administration, University of Hong Kong.

Glatter R and Woods P A (1993) *Competitive Arenas in Education: Studying the Impact of Enhanced Competition and Choice on Parents and Schools* Paper presented to Conference 'Quasi-Markets: The Emerging Findings', University of Bristol, March.

Glatter R, Johnson D and Woods P A (1993) 'Marketing, choice and responses in education' in Smith M (ed) *Managing Schools in an Uncertain Environment: Resources, Marketing and Power* Sheffield, Sheffield Hallam University for BEMAS (British Educational Management and Administration Society).

Goldring E B and Bauch P A (1993) *Parental Involvement and School Responsiveness: Facilitating the Home–School Connection in Schools of Choice* Paper presented at the Annual Meeting of the American Educational Research Association, Atlanta, April 1993.

HM Inspector of Schools (1992) *Using Ethos Indicators in Secondary School Self-Evaluation: Taking Account of the Views of Pupils, Parents and Teachers*, Edinburgh, Scottish Office Education Department.

Jones G, Bastiani J, Bell G and Chapman C (1992) *A Willing Partnership* London, RSA and NAHT.

Levacic R (1992) 'The LEA and its schools: the decentralized organization and the internal market' in Wallace G (ed) *Local Management of Schools: Research and Experience, BERA Dialogues,* Clevedon, Multilingual Matters.

Levacic R (1993) *Towards Understanding and Evaluating the Performance of Quasi-Markets: The Experience of the State School Sector in England and Wales 1988–1992* Paper presented to Conference 'Quasi-Markets: The Emerging Findings', University of Bristol, March.

Levacic R and Woods P A (1994) 'New Forms of Financial Co-operation' in Ranson S and Tomlinson J (eds) *New Models in School Co-operation* London, Longman.

Macbeth A (1989) *Involving Parents* Oxford, Heinemann Educational.

Merttens R and Vass J (eds) (1993) *Partnerships in Maths* London, Falmer Press.

Mesley W R (1991) 'Bold development of community and business links by Sandhurst primaries' in *Berkshire County Council News* No 2, Reading, Berkshire County Council.

Morris R (1993) *Choice of School: A Survey 1992–93* London, Association of Metropolitan Authorities.

Morris R and Fowler J (1993) *Beyond Clause Zero: The Education Bill 1992–93* London, Association of Metropolitan Authorities.

South Bristol Federation (1992) *Federation Principles* (folder), Bristol, South Bristol Federation.

Thompson G, Frances, J, Levacic, R and Mitchell, J (eds) (1991) *Markets, Hierarchies and Networks* London, Sage.

Weeks R (1992) 'Staffroom SWOT' *Education*, 25 September.

Woods P A (1992) 'Changing schools' *Management in Education*, 6, 1, pp 11–13.

Woods P A (1993a) 'Parents as consumer-citizens' in Merttens R, Mayers D, Brown A and Vass J (eds) *Ruling the Margins: Problematising Parental Involvement* IMPACT Project, London, University of North London Press.

Woods P A (1993b) 'Responding to the consumer: parental choice and school effectiveness' *School Effectiveness and School Improvement*, 4, 3.

Chapter 10

Weak Choice, Strong Choice, and the New Christian Schools

Geoffrey Walford

The majority of recent research and debate about educational choice has been in terms of families selecting particular schools for their children from the range on offer. For most parents this means expressing a preference between the various state-maintained schools in their vicinity. Families are expected to make judgements about such factors as academic success, discipline, facilities and distance to be travelled, and then act tactically to try to ensure that the child is offered a place at a school that they consider acceptable. Tickell (1980) has defined this a 'weak' choice, for families are only able to express preferences about what is already on offer. It is like choosing from a menu at a restaurant. If grilled salmon is not on the menu then it cannot be ordered.

Thus, with secondary schools, families are able to choose among their local county schools, voluntary aided schools and/or grant-maintained schools, but they have little say in determining the range or nature of what is locally available. Not only do they have to make their choices in the knowledge that popular schools may become oversubscribed and be unable to accept the child, but they may also perceive all the schools on offer to be unsatisfactory. For these families 'weak' choice is seen as insufficient, and there is a growing demand for 'strong' choice where families can help shape the choices on offer, and can establish schools which meet their own specific requirements. At present 'strong' choice is only available in Britain within the private sector, and various groups of parents have found themselves reluctantly forced into the private sector to obtain or establish a school which matches their religious or philosophical beliefs (Walford, 1991).

Most of those seeking 'strong' choice wish to have schools that reflect their religious beliefs. They perceive that mainstream Church of England and Roman Catholic families already have this right and ask that the right be extended to cover other religious groups. There is considerable power to their argument. Since the 1944 Education Act the vast majority of religious denominational primary and secondary schools in England and Wales have been an integral part of the state-maintained system as voluntary schools. These schools have all of their everyday running costs and teachers' salaries provided by the state, while (in the case of voluntary-aided schools) the church organizations pay 15 per cent of any new capital expenditure required. At present about 28 per cent of primary-aged pupils and 17 per cent of secondary pupils are in voluntary schools. Of the overall total of about 22 per cent of pupils, about 11 per cent are in Church of England schools, 9 per cent in Roman Catholic schools and 0.1 per cent or less in each of Jewish and Methodist schools. Additionally, nearly 2 per cent of pupils are in non-religious voluntary schools which were originally established by charities, guilds or individual founders (see O'Keeffe, 1986).

But these current arrangements leave some groups highly dissatisfied, for they reflect the social and religious character of the 1940s rather than the 1990s. As Britain has gradually become more multi-ethnic and more diverse, there has been growing pressure to establish schools to serve these new groups. In theory, there are clear procedures for the establishment of new voluntary schools and it is open to the followers of other Christian denominations or religious faiths to propose schools which could be incorporated within the state-maintained system. Yet, in practice, in spite of clear demand for such schools from some groups, there are currently no Muslim or Hindu schools in the state sector. Neither are there any state supported schools representing any of the smaller or less-traditional Christian groups or denominations.

There are several reasons for this situation. The first is demographic, for increased pressure for new schools has occurred at a time of dramatically falling school rolls, such that local education authorities have concentrated their attention on closing existing schools rather than supporting new ones. A second reason is that there is widespread unease about the idea of Muslim schools. In part, this is due to fears that an Islamic understanding of the role of women may be in conflict with the Western view of equal opportunities, but it also relates to a fear of fundamentalism of all shades. The continuing Salman Rushdie affair, with its book-burning imagery, has done little to help the cause of Muslim schools. Power to create new voluntary schools is vested in the local education authorities and the Secretary of State for Education, all of whom have preferred to avoid controversy and have generally refused applications for voluntary status on criteria officially unrelated to the religious basis of the proposed schools. As a result, some Muslim, Orthodox Jewish, Seventh Day Adventist and evangelical Christian parents, in particular, have felt compelled to start their own private schools to enable their own worldview to be taught (Walford, 1991).

Evangelical Christian Schools

One of the most interesting groups of private schools where parents are exercising strong choice is the new Christian schools. These schools share an ideology of biblically based evangelical Christianity which seeks to relate the message of the Bible to all aspects of present day life whether personal, spiritual or educational. These schools have usually been set up by parents or a church group to deal with a growing dissatisfaction with what is seen as the increased secularism of the great majority of schools. The schools aim to provide a distinctive Christian approach to every part of school life and the curriculum and, in most cases, parents have a continuing role in the management and organisation of the schools.

As there is no national organisation overseeing these schools, it is difficult to trace their emergence, but it would appear that the first school of this type to open in Britain was in Rochester in 1969. A few more new Christian schools followed in the early 1970s, but it was not until the early 1980s that substantial growth occurred. In 1980 there were about 10 such schools, but by 1992 there were nearly 90. The growth in popularity of these schools is shown in the increase in the number of pupils in each school as well as the total number of schools. Several schools which opened with just a handful of pupils have rapidly increased to cater for over 100 (Deakin, 1989). The main constraint on further expansion for many of these schools is a limitation in the physical space available in the existing premises rather than any lack of potential pupils. The demand for places must be understood in the light of evangelical Christianity at present being one of the fastest growing religious groups in Britain.

For several reasons the exact number of schools is difficult to determine. One factor is that the number is continually changing as new schools open and existing ones close, but more important is the lack of any strict definition of what should count as a new Christian school or overall organisation representing the schools. Some schools are linked to small Christian sects, and have no wish to be associated with any other school. Others believe their own situation is very different from the majority of new Christian schools, and do not believe there is any benefit to be gained from associating with them.

About 65 of these schools have, however, come together through mutual recognition into a loose grouping through the Christian Schools Trust. As the number of schools increased during the 1980s, several of the heads of the schools began to meet together regularly but informally for Christian fellowship and to discuss matters of mutual interest. More formal meetings and some conferences began to be held, and other teaching staff became involved such that, by 1988, a decision was made to establish a separate Christian Schools Trust (CST) 'to promote and assist in the founding of further schools' (CST, 1988). The Trust also provides assistance in the development of curriculum materials, helps coordinate the dissemination of such materials, provides some in-service training for teachers and organises conferences.

This chapter is principally concerned with schools which have an association with the CST, and the data presented here is derived from a larger study of these schools (Poyntz and Walford, 1994). A selection of 11 of these schools were visited and the heads were interviewed using a semi-structured format. In early 1993, a questionnaire was sent to the rest of the schools listed by the CST. Reminders and second questionnaires were subsequently sent to those who did not initially respond, and data were eventually obtained from 83 per cent of the schools in the group. Documents were also collected and analysed. Although there is variety within the schools involved with the CST, the image the Trust presents tends to be that of charismatic Christianity where considerable emphasis is given to the gifts of the Holy Spirit such as 'speaking in tongues' and 'healing'. New Christian schools without such an emphasis thus tend not to be included.

The survey found that the schools ranged considerably in size from fewer than 10 to nearly 200 children, with a total of more than 3,000 children in the 53 schools responding to the survey. About half of the schools cater for primary-age children only, but the rest usually teach the full compulsory school-age range up to 16. Most of the schools were started either by churches or by groups of Christian parents and are designed to enable parents to provide a 'biblically based' Christian education for their children. The majority of the pupils are thus sons or daughters of active Christians, but most of the schools are also prepared to accept a proportion of pupils from non-Christian families. This includes a very small proportion of pupils from Muslim, Hindu or Sikh families. As one of the examples below indicates, a few of the schools were established with Christian evangelism as an explicit aim, and accept a large proportion of pupils from non-Christian families.

In the main, these schools are not well funded and do not serve traditional social-class users of the private sector. A few do charge fees that compare with other private preparatory or secondary schools and are able to provide full salaries to teachers at the nationally agreed levels. But the majority of the schools have low indicative fees or rely on donations from parents that are related to their ability to pay. These schools often live a life of financial uncertainty or, as they would explain it, the schools survive 'on faith'. Most of the schools had a mixture of full and part-time teachers with those working part-time often being parents and receiving no pay at all. Of those teachers working full-time about 20 per cent received no payment, sometimes because they did not require any additional family income or sometimes because they 'lived by faith' and relied on voluntary gifts from parents, the church or others. Where teachers were paid, the majority were on salaries lower than that they would have obtained in the state sector.

The flavour and diversity of the schools is best understood through a few example descriptions. The following accounts are not selected to be 'typical', but to indicate range and variability. The first example is one of the larger schools within the group which opened in September 1984 with 24 children, and now has expanded to cater for about 130 children aged between 5 and 16. Its 100 primary-age pupils are housed in a redundant 1950s church, situated in a council housing estate. The buildings have been adapted and renovated to provide classrooms, offices, hall, staffroom and so on, and now look very similar to many state maintained primary schools. The facilities are of a reasonable standard, but the school is not lavishly equipped. It does not provide the form of elite education often associated with private schools. This school was established by a group of four local biblically based evangelical Christian fellowships and serves families of mixed social-class origins. It provides an education which revolves around the desire to teach children to grow in a personal relationship with God. Its curriculum is integrated and topic based rather than subject based. Within the overall topic of Justice and Righteousness, for example, the top juniors might study the Stewardship of Creation, including pollution of the environment, destruction of rain forests and similar issues. The focus is on the child knowing God, knowing His created world and knowing other people. The school has six full-time staff, about six others sharing classes on a morning or afternoon basis, and about 20 more part-time staff. Although the school has a few children from non-Christian families, the majority are from families within the local fellowships. The general expectation is that parents with children at the school will donate 10 per cent of their income, but this does not allow teachers to be paid full salaries. Payment to teaching staff is thus made according to need.

A second school linked to the CST provides a clear contrast. It is situated in an area with a large local Asian population, and the majority of the 120 primary-age pupils at the school are from Muslim, Hindu or Sikh families. Only 10 per cent are from Christian homes. Yet all the teachers are Christian, and the head's aim is that the school should provide 'a good education and a Christian education'. The school has set fees which allow the staff to be paid on the same salary scale as teachers in the state system. Non-Christian parents choose this school for their children because of its ordered and disciplined environment and because they prefer their children to be in a religiously based school (even if it is not their own), rather than the secular one of the local state-maintained schools.

The school uses an old church building and is reasonably spacious, with most of the classes in separate rooms. However, two of the classes have to share a large hall separated from one another by temporary room dividers. At playtime the children walk to the local park some 10 minutes away. The Christian emphasis is evident in all areas of school life, and is reflected in the wall posters with Bible quotations that decorate the classroom walls. In interview the head emphasised the importance of the creation story to his understanding of the Christian message and has recently spent a considerable time speaking about Genesis chapter 1 in the school assemblies.

A rather different sub-group of schools within the CST group have a controversial history, and suffered badly in the press following poor reports from HM Inspectors during 1985 when at least four new Christian schools were served with notices of complaint. Areas of concern within these reports included inadequate and unsafe accommodation, lack of resources, unstimulating environments, and inadequate curricula. In all four reports, however, the Accelerated Christian Education (ACE) teaching programme used by the schools was a common area of concern.

ACE teaching materials and methods were an important part of the growth of some of these new Christian schools, for the existence of ACE enabled small groups of Christian parents to contemplate providing all-age Christian schooling for their children at low cost and with little or no teaching experience required by those adults in charge. According to the survey, about a third of the schools in the group make significant use of ACE materials, and a few use little else. ACE is also important where Christian families are geographically isolated, for about 100 families use it as the foundation of their home-schooling of their children.

As explained in detail elsewhere (Walford, 1991), ACE is a highly standardised system of individualised instruction developed in the United States, where all the information, materials and equipment necessary to set up and run a school are provided. According to Rose (1988), by about 1987 ACE was used in 5,000 schools in the United States and a further 600 schools in 86 other countries. Rose describes ACE as

> having taken the scientific management of schools to the extreme. Their model more closely approximates to that of the factory or office: there are 'supervisors' and 'monitors' rather than 'teachers'; student 'offices' rather than desks; and 'testing stations' that create 'quality control'. (1988, p 117)

Pupils work on their individual Packs of Accelerated Christian Education (PACEs) in separate cubicles, which are designed to limit student interaction by having vertical screens between pupils. Students are able to gain the attention of their supervisor or monitor by raising one of two or three small flags which are provided for each pupil.

In practice, the heavy criticism of the method from HMIs and others has meant that many of the newer schools in the group have never used

ACE. Schools are now involved in developing their own materials and, even where used, in most schools ACE methods no longer dominate the learning process. However, some of the schools associated with the Trust still see ACE as central to their vision of Christian education, and believe that its emphasis on ordered independent learning rather than whole-class teaching reflects and reinforces Christian discipline and the Christian message.

Why Start a School?

It is striking that the new Christian schools are the result of grass-roots movements in education which stem from the belief that education is the responsibility of the parent and the church rather than the state. For example, in its prospectus, one of the schools stated this as:

> The basic responsibility for education lies with parents. The well known proverb 'Train a child the way he should go, and when he is old he will not turn from it' (Proverbs 22:6) is addressed primarily to parents. There are regular parents' meetings to encourage a close relationship between home and school.

The school is seen as an extension of the values and beliefs taught within the home and church. Deakin (1989), who was Head of one of the schools, argues that the human-centred philosophy which dominates the majority of schools in the UK is evident throughout the entire curriculum of those schools, and that it shapes the value systems and philosophical frameworks within which all the disciplines are taught. Further:

> our schools tend to reflect our society, where there is increasing secularisation, a rising materialism and excessive individualism. Alongside this there is unremitting evidence of a profound lack of respect for authority, and chaos in the area of personal values and morality.

Religious education itself is often of particular concern to the parents involved in these schools. It is argued that the secularisation of most schools has led to a commitment to a multi-faith approach to religious education, where religions are examined through their observable characteristics rather than in terms of faith, belief and commitment. This approach is seen to encourage a secular and aridly sceptical view of life and to devalue all faiths other than that of secular humanism.

Such a view was common to all those interviewed. For example, one respondent explained the perceived need for a specifically Christian school in the following way:

> We believe in a Christ-centred curriculum. That there should not be a split, a divide, between the home and family and the school – that their education should be an extension of what they learn at home. We obviously have Christ and the Bible at the centre at home, and we want them to have the same at school.
>
> I think the divide between Christian education and state education has become far, far greater over recent years – humanism is taught. And not only in the curriculum, but in terms of what children learn in the playground ...

Interviews with heads and others involved in setting up schools showed that there was considerable variety in the precipitating reasons and in the processes by which they had been established. This was explained in greater detail by one well-informed head:

> At one time a lot of Christian schools started because there was a lot happening in other schools that Christians weren't happy with. So there were the obvious things such as halloween, some of the areas of sex education, obvious areas of RE, obvious areas of worship, evolution, creation. And parents would say this is causing concern. I mean, I could give you a list of things that have happened even recently, and locally. We've had children in schools where they've had a whole day given over to fortune telling. We've had children putting needles into dolls ... There are schools where they've been making prayer mats and praying to monkey gods. Now these are clear things that as Christians we get concerned about and object about. We also object that evolution is taught as a fact and not as a theory ...
>
> The Bible says that we should train up our children in the way they should go ... I don't have to have a special reason to put my children, as a father, in a Christian school. For I am simply doing what God wants me to do – to train the children up – my children – in the way that they should go. Everything is based on God's will.

Now how could I obey that command to train up my children the way they should go when so much of their five day a week schooling is against those standards or at the very least is not based on them? So for that positive reason I need to put my children in a place where the standards and attitudes and the ethos are in sympathy with what I would teach at home. It is the family, church and school that work together for the child ...

So there are very positive ways why the school started. We always share it with parents in terms of two Ps. It is Protection, but not in a negative sense. All good parents will put the medicines out of the way, they will put the stair-gate on, they will put the safety belts on in the car, and then, often, they will let them go to school without any sense of protection. And the second P is Preparation. We prepare them to be full citizens in all ways. If they want their faith developing we help them with that, but we clearly try to develop them to at least be aware of all the different debates and standards that they need to be aware of when they leave school.

Conclusion

Once implemented, the 1993 Education Act will allow a wider range of voluntary bodies to start new grant-maintained schools. As long as they are prepared to accept certain regulations, the way has been opened for schools run by evangelical Christians, Muslims, Hindus or other religious groups. Such new grant-maintained schools will have to teach the National Curriculum, be open to children of all faiths, and have a more broadly based governing body than many of them have at present, but in return, they will receive state funding for all their recurrent costs and 85 per cent of initial capital expenditure. Since the new Christian schools have been active in campaigning for such a change (Walford, 1991), several now have plans to make applications to re-establish themselves as new grant-maintained schools.

The idea that the state should fund a variety of different schools according to parents' wishes has a powerful simplicity which has welded together a remarkable range of people and organisations from the political right and left. Freedom of choice has become a powerful ideological force – but it is one that has been used to partly conceal the

New Right's political objective of a more individualistic and inequitable educational system. At an individual level, it is perfectly right and proper that parents should wish to make choices on behalf of their children for their perceived benefit. A good parent will wish his or her own children to receive the best education that is available. But what is good for the individual is not always good for society as a whole or for certain less privileged groups or individuals within that society. Individual choices, and the sum effect of individual choices, may have benefits for those making choices, but may also harm others who are less able or willing to participate in the choice-making process (Walford, 1993). The presence of private schools, for example, may harm state schools by taking out from the state sector those parents who are most likely to ensure that high standards of provision and teaching are maintained. The education provided in state schools may thus deteriorate with the exit of those parents with the greatest concern or financial resources. However, it is the duty of the state to ensure that the less privileged and less powerful are not harmed by the actions of the more privileged and more powerful – a duty which may mean that individual freedoms are constrained for the benefit of the society as a whole.

In practice, much of the present Conservative government's educational policy will increase injustice and inequity, and lead to a hierarchy of schools which will provide very different educational experiences for children of different abilities, social classes and ethnic groups. Whether all the participants recognise it or not, the new 1993 legislation giving state funding to Christian and other religiously based schools is part of this wider political programme.

The solution is not straightforward, for there needs to be a balance between the desires of individuals and society's need to ensure that schools do not become elitist or segregationist. The Christian schools are not themselves elitist. Some of them currently serve children from the most deserving segments of our society, and most of them are prepared to accept a small number of non-Christian children where they have room. Furthermore, the schools have good grounds for asking for state support, as some 22 per cent of children in state maintained schools are already in religious denominational schools. In the interests of equity, it is necessary to allow other voluntary bodies to establish state-maintained schools, but the most appropriate way of doing this is through the LEAs rather than by any new type of grant-maintained or voluntary school. To prevent schools becoming elitist or segregationist these new schools should be under the general supervision of the LEAs, and should work in cooperation with other schools. They should have their own ethos and cover such additional areas as they see fit beyond the National Curriculum. LEAs would act to monitor and maintain standards and to ensure that no religious or cultural entry conditions were imposed. Such conditions would be too strict for some of the Christian schools to accept, but they are necessary if an equitable education system is to be available to all children.

Acknowledgements

I am most grateful to the Nuffield Foundation for a grant to support this research, and to Colin Poyntz for his help in the preparation of this paper.

References

CST (1988) *Information Sheet* Christian Schools Trust

Deakin, R (1989) *The New Christian Schools* Bristol, Regius Press.

Department of Education and Science (1985) *Report by HM Inspectors on New Court Christian School, Finsbury Park, London* (176/85), London, DES.

O'Keeffe, B (1986) *Faith, Culture and the Dual System*, Lewes, Falmer Press.

Poyntz, C and Walford, G (1994) 'The new Christian schools: a survey' *Educational Studies* (forthcoming).

Rose, Susan D (1988) *Keeping them out of the Hands of Satan: Evangelical Schooling in America* London, Routledge & Kegan Paul.

Tickell, G (1980) *Choice in Education* Canberra, Australian Schools Commission.

Walford, G (1991) 'The reluctant private sector: of small schools, politics and people' in Walford, G (ed) *Private Schooling: Tradition, Change and Diversity* London, Paul Chapman.

Walford, G (1993) *Choice and Equity in Education* London, Cassell.

Chapter 11

Parents who Choose to Educate their Children at Home

Jean Bendell

In Britain, education is compulsory for children aged 5 to 16. Most people understand this to mean that children have to go to school. However, even though such phrases as 'compulsory school age' are used, the law recognises that education and school are not synonymous terms. It is education which is compulsory, not school. There is an alternative to school attendance and this usually involves parents taking on the education of their children themselves at home. Although it is by no means a new phenomenon, it has been chosen by increasing numbers of parents in recent years.

Legal Aspects of Home Education

The Parents' Charter (Department of Education and Science, 1991), while accepting that parents have rights in matters such as preference for a particular school or for their chosen school to opt out of local authority control, fails to mention that parents have rights of a far more fundamental nature. First, they can legally choose to educate their children themselves. The law throughout the UK accepts that parents are responsible for their children's education. Section 36 of the 1944 Education Act for England and Wales, as amended by the 1981 Education Act, states:

> It shall be the duty of the parent of every child of compulsory school age to cause him to receive efficient full-time education

suitable to his age, ability and aptitude, and to any special educational needs he may have, either by regular attendance at school or otherwise.

The Education (Northern Ireland) Act, 1947 and the Scottish Education Act 1980 contain parallel sections. It is this key phrase 'or otherwise' which enables parents to make the choice of educating their children at home. It is from this wording that the Education Otherwise movement has taken its name.

Second, parents have the right to have their children educated 'in conformity with their own religious and philosophical convictions' (Protocol to the European Convention for the Protection of Human Rights and Fundamental Freedoms, Article 2, March 1952). The Protocol, ratified by Britain, supports the principle that the state must respect the rights of parents regarding the nature of their children's education. This obligation of the state is also made clear in Section 76 of the 1944 Education Act (see Chapter 2).

It should be noted that the ability of parents to choose to educate their children otherwise than through attendance at school is a legal right, not a loophole. It is not something about which parents have to avoid detection or for which they need to be granted special permission in order to proceed. If their children have never been to a state school, they are not even obliged to alert the LEA and declare their intentions. The situation is less straightforward for parents who wish to withdraw their children from school. These children must first be deregistered (see below).

Parents should bear in mind, however, that it is the duty of the LEA to ensure that all children in their area are receiving 'efficient full-time education' (Section 36, 1944 Education Act). The LEA is empowered to serve notice on parents who appear to be failing to ensure their children are being properly educated. Such parents are then obliged to satisfy the authority that they are carrying out the duty imposed on them in Section 36. Failure to do so can result in a school attendance order or, ultimately, if it is considered necessary in order to ensure that the children are being educated, a care order. The prospect of such measures alarms many parents who are contemplating home education. Nevertheless, it should be stressed that the vast majority of parents who have decided to undertake their children's education themselves do not encounter such problems.

As more parents have decided on home education, LEAs have drawn up procedures which deal with them reasonably and without recourse to expensive legal proceedings. In the past, when there were fewer parents choosing the 'otherwise' option, LEAs were sometimes high-handed in their treatment of them. Consequently, there were some well-publicised legal battles over home education (for example, see Baker, 1964). During the past decade or so, for a number of reasons, there has been a growth in public awareness that learning at home is a legal alternative to school. This is perhaps partly due to the work of the organisation Education Otherwise, a support group for home-educating families, and to publications aimed to make known to parents their right to keep responsibility for their children's education (Holt, 1981; Bendell, 1987). It is perhaps partly also the result of keen media interest in individual exceptionally talented children, a number of whom have been educated by their parents (for example, see Deakin, 1972). It is probably also due to changes introduced by government in this period. These have not only directly affected the way children are taught in schools and the way schools are run but also, arguably, have brought about a shift in people's perception of educational provision as a public service. Consumer rights are now a central issue in education. *The Parents' Charter* assures parents of their right to choose: many are now looking at the schools on offer with a critical eye – and some are choosing to opt out.

Parents who intend to withdraw a child from school should write to the headteacher and request that his or her name is removed from the roll. Deregistration is necessary because the law requires that if a child is registered at a school then he or she must attend it regularly (Section 39, 1944 Education Act). It is the parents' duty to ensure that the child does so. The question of deregistration only arises where a child is being withdrawn from a state school. It is not an issue for families if their children have never been to school – even if they are on a particular school's waiting list – or if they have attended a private school. Deregistration is not necessary for families returning from abroad. (Fuller information on deregistration and other legal aspects of withdrawing a child from school is given in Deutsch and Wolf, 1991.)

Before turning to the question of why parents might choose to educate their children at home – and why some people are so opposed to the idea – a few common myths should be dispelled about the obligations that the law places on such parents. It has sometimes been incorrectly assumed that parents can only educate their children at home if they are qualified teachers or if they employ tutors. This is not true. Furthermore, they are not required by law to provide the LEA with timetables or details of a parallel to schooling – even though they may be asked to do so. They are not required to adhere to the National Curriculum. Education at home does not need to take place in a classroom or similar setting and does not need to consist of formal lessons.

The procedures drawn up by LEAs for dealing with the increasing numbers of families involved in home-based education have often involved ready-printed forms which may routinely ask for timetables, curricula or even testimonials regarding the parents' suitability as educators. Parents do not have to comply with requests to provide such information. However, some feel it is reasonable to do so and that it will help to maintain an amicable relationship with the LEA. Some parents choose to follow the guidelines of the National Curriculum, not only to comply with the possible expectations of the LEA but also to ensure that their children are keeping up with their school-educated peers. Other parents may decide that timetables and curricula are inappropriate, that the very notion of breaking down the process of learning into a set number of subjects and hours of instruction is incompatible with the aims of home education. It is possible to have such an argument accepted and even approved by an LEA, without confrontation.

Education Otherwise

Education Otherwise – familiarly known as EO – is a self-help organisation run by and for families practising or interested in home-based education. Formed early in 1977 by a small group of parents, it has grown steadily to its current membership of about 2,500. As a network of families spread across Britain in cities as well as in rural areas, it is able to provide advice and information drawing on many individual experiences over a number of years. It has a small number of members abroad as well as links with Growing Without Schooling, an organisation for home educators in the USA.

EO is a registered charity, without any source of income other than from members' subscriptions, donations and the sale of publications. Its existence depends on the commitment and unpaid work of its members, some of whom undertake jobs at local or national level. In each area there is a coordinator, usually a parent with experience of home education with school-age children. The coordinator deals with enquirers and new members, drawing on the fund of expertise provided by a national network of home-educating families.

For those contemplating or practising home education, EO is often a good source of support. It aims to offer a service to its members and to establish the right of families to make responsible choices about education. EO organises national events, including conferences, residential weekends and meetings. It provides members with a contact list, a newsletter issued six times a year, a guide to the legal aspects of education other than through regular attendance at school and two source books containing ideas for learning at home, one for younger children and the other for the teen years.

Membership is open to everyone, with or without home-educated children. It is perhaps especially valuable for those starting out on home education, whatever the age of the child. Deciding to undertake a child's education – particularly when it involves withdrawing him or her from the school system – seems to many parents to be a daunting step into unknown territory. Parents often find it very heartening to know that other families, who had once faced similar problems and had similar decisions to make, have successfully taken the step. Ideas and accounts of members' experiences are exchanged through the newsletter. Many of EO's members use its contact list to meet like-minded families locally or further afield. Apart from the national meetings, members may also arrange local social and educational events. Additionally, the contact list is useful for those wishing to trade skills or resources.

EO's members have chosen education at home – or support the idea of home-based education – for many different reasons. Among its members, there is a wide diversity of lifestyles and views. EO does not set out to recommend any particular method of teaching or to provide its members with materials or syllabuses. Since it draws its membership from a variety of backgrounds, no one view of home education would be acceptable to all. It is an association of people with the common aim of supporting families who choose to keep – rather than to delegate – responsibility for the education of their children.

World-wide Education Service

The World-wide Education Service (WES) was set up to help families avoid separation when a parent is employed overseas in a country where suitable education facilities may not be available. It is an offshoot of the Parents' National Education Union (PNEU), a charity founded by the Victorian educationalist, Charlotte Mason. Their Home School programme was designed for parents to use when teaching their children themselves, thus avoiding the separation which would result from boarding schools. The programme is intended to give the equivalent of a 'good' school education for children up to the age of 13. After this age, children would be expected to go to school in time to start work on public examination syllabuses.

Although the WES Home School programme was developed for use by expatriate families, it is also used by some parents in the UK who feel the need for a correspondence course and advisory support for teaching their school-age children. It involves the 'creation of a school in the home', based on a structured system of education. This approach is acceptable to some parents who teach their children themselves, perhaps especially those who see home education as an alternative to private schooling.

Reasons why Parents choose Home Education

One source in EO half-humorously observed that there are two broad groups of home educators: those with a philosophy and those with a problem. Although a simplification, there is some truth in this. There are, of course, many widely differing philosophies and a variety of problems which might lead parents to decide on education at home rather than at school. There may also be an overlap between the two groups. However, this distinction serves as a starting point for considering some of the common reasons parents give for choosing home education for their children.

Looking first at the philosophies, a political basis may be identified in some of the arguments put forward. The term 'deschoolers' has been used of advocates of home education, particularly of those who are critical not just of the school system but of the function of school in society as a whole. In his book *Deschooling Society*, Illich (1971) proposes that schooling plays an important role in perpetuating and strengthening inequality. He sees it as a global problem, noting its impact on third world countries. He observes that disadvantaged people often find themselves judged as failures according to educational measures which have, arguably, been set up to exclude them.

Some supporters of home education assert that schooling in Britain has a similar insidious function and that this function is detrimental to the development of the majority of children. It was the aim of the 1944 Education Act to give children greater equality of opportunity. For the first time in Britain free secondary education was made available to all. This was seen as opening the way for poorer children into higher education. However, two decades after the Act's implementation, the Robbins Report (1963) noted that the proportion of working class boys at university was no higher than it had been in the 1930s.

It can be observed that more recent educational reforms have done even less to challenge the power structure of Britain. The country is still run by an elite which, largely, has been privately educated. Only 7 per cent of pupils have access to private schooling and yet they account for 40 per cent of all entrants to Oxford and Cambridge. A high proportion of those in the most influential and highly paid jobs have had a public school education: the figures are over 80 per cent for High Court judges, directors of clearing banks, Anglican bishops and army personnel of the rank of Major-General or above (Boyd, 1973; Griggs, 1985). These figures have remained remarkably constant over the past 40 years.

As a result of changes in state education funding in recent years, a third tier seems to be evolving out of the traditional two-tier system. There has always been a potential gap between the facilities available in private schools and in state schools. In the private sector – or the independent sector as its supporters now like it to be called – class sizes may be smaller (Griggs, 1985) and classrooms may be better endowed in terms of resources, such as additional specialist teachers and facilities for science, sports and music. There are indications that there is now a growing gap in facilities between popular state schools, especially those in better-off areas where parents may be actively and financially involved in the running of local schools, and the less popular schools, where reduction in funding is likely to lead to a cycle of neglect and decline.

Even within the same school, there appear to be mechanisms which work to the disadvantage of less-privileged children. Douglas (1964) showed that working class children were more likely to find themselves in lower streams, doing less well in tests after their years of junior schooling and faring even worse where selection for secondary schools was based on interviews and teacher assessments. The issue of teacher expectation and its effects is a recurring theme in writings about classroom achievement. Concepts such as the self-fulfilling prophecy (Rosenthal and Jacobson, 1968), the structure of power within schools and the cultural bias of instruction and assessments have been put forward to explain the relative underachievement of those who are working class, female or West Indian.

Some home educators decide to turn their backs on the 'qualification-escalation ratchet' (Dore, 1976), a mechanism which ensures that more qualifications and higher grades are increasingly being required of today's school-leavers as competition grows for jobs, higher education and training places. As greater numbers of school-leavers fail to find openings for the careers for which their qualifications would formerly have made them eligible, they turn instead to the jobs which are available. In time their higher standard of qualifications becomes the standard for these lower status jobs. As more qualifications are needed before a school-leaver can embark on certain careers, it looks as if only the most intelligent and able are being selected. A school system which appears to give equal opportunity to all hides the role it plays itself in maintaining that inequality. Some deschoolers believe that schooling should be seen as the means whereby these inequalities are perpetuated and – more significantly – are also justified. In opting out of the paper chase for qualifications, some parents choose instead to equip their children with a different outlook on life, one based on skills and resourcefulness rather than on the ability to pass examinations. For some families, the 'otherwise' option may be chosen as part of an alternative lifestyle. For others, the decision may be made on religious grounds. They may consider that local schools will not offer the guidance and moral training which they feel is important. They may disagree with the content of what is taught in schools.

There are a number of arguments for home education which focus on the effect of schooling on children themselves. Some parents maintain that children lose their curiosity and willingness to learn when confined to a classroom all day. It is certainly notable that children who learn at home do not generally need the long hours of daily instruction that they would receive in schools. Home education may give them opportunities to learn at their own rate, to follow their own interests and to enjoy more hours of leisure. Some parents may feel that childhood is not the time to be cooped up and coerced into learning.

At home, adult attention is likely to be shared among far fewer children: tuition may be possible on a one-to-one or similar basis. It may consequently be less didactic in style, encouraging more questions and more active participation than is usual in a classroom setting. The education received need not be limited by the demands of the National Curriculum or by the expected rate of progress of the average child. Parents may see the advantages of this for their individual children, perhaps especially those whose children are exceptionally able or who have learning difficulties. Some parents choose home education because of dissatisfaction over the assessment their child has received for a Statement of Special Educational Needs or over the provision that their LEA offers. They may see particular benefits for their less-advantaged children to grow up and learn in a supportive family environment.

Perhaps a greater number of parents choose home education because of their children's problems at school rather than initially through their philosophical convictions. Bullying has been one of the most common reasons that parents give for withdrawing a child from school. Parents may be especially dismayed not only to learn that their child has been bullied but also, in some cases, to find that it is the victim rather than the perpetrator of bullying who may be treated unsympathetically by teachers. For some families, education at home is seen as the solution to school phobia. Children may be unhappy at school for a variety of reasons. They may feel bored, unable to keep up with the work, socially isolated and unable to mix with their classmates. Learning at home – not necessarily permanently – may give them the space and time they need to sort out their problems.

One of the reasons for the recent increase in the number of parents choosing home education may be a knock-on effect of the recession. Some parents who have unexpectedly found themselves unable to afford private education have preferred to educate their children themselves rather than send them to local state schools. For some of these parents home education may be seen as a stop-gap measure. Unemployment also enables some to consider options which would not have been practicable when they were full-time wage earners. Education at home usually entails a considerable commitment from parents in terms of time.

Common Arguments against Home Education

Some people argue that competition is essential for children's development and that schools encourage this. However, families who opt for learning at home may see competitiveness as a negative aspect of schooling. They may have seen their children pay a heavy price for their success at school or they may feel that those who do not have a chance of being successful may give up the struggle. They may not wish their children to accept the labels that a competitive system places on them.

The idea that schools offer children wider opportunities is one that is often put forward by critics of home education. As discussed earlier, it may be argued that the structure of British society is maintained by the varying quality of education that is on offer – in separate schools – for different social classes. Additionally, even within the same school, the amount of progress made by a pupil may vary according to class, gender and ethnic group. Furthermore, since career prospects are linked to educational qualifications, school can be seen as one of a series of hurdles largely designed to keep the less privileged out of the best jobs. Home education may be doing nothing to redress the imbalance but some home educators prefer to feel that they are opting out of such a system.

Concern is sometimes expressed that a family environment cannot provide the facilities which are thought to be essential for the teaching of certain subjects at school. The sciences are often seen to be a particular problem, requiring not only expensive equipment which would not be found in most homes but also specialist knowledge which many parents lack. Would-be home-educating parents often worry about their inability to provide their children with a good broad education. It is a worry which sometimes evaporates in the early years as they see how quickly children can learn when they are interested and are able to progress at their own pace. Parents also report that they learn a great deal themselves as they go along and that, especially in the early years, there is not the need for expensive equipment. They may point out that their local schools are underfunded and poorly equipped. Many home educators believe that it is more important to foster an eagerness for learning than to teach children a particular set of facts which may only have relevance in a classroom setting.

However, it may be a worry which re-emerges in the later secondary-school years, especially if pressure is on to cover a large number of subjects for GCSEs. It is here that some parents may need to call on outside help, in the form of correspondence courses or expert tuition. Of course, home education does not need to be a permanent arrangement: many children who have been educated at home later go to school and perform well academically.

People who initially express concern about home education often accept quite readily that children can and do learn out of school. They may even accept that learning may be more rapid away from the distractions and the constraints of a classroom. The concern more commonly expressed, as reported by some home educators (see Bendell, 1987), is that children who do not have to go to school will fail to be socialised. It is widely assumed that children need to go to school in order to learn how to mix with other people. It may be argued in response to this that the type of socialisation that children get in school prepares them for school and for little else. The classroom social set-up – 30 or so children herded together for long periods of the day simply because they are in the same age group – has its own peculiarities. Certainly, though, any parents considering letting their children learn at home must also give thought as to how they are going to meet their children's social needs.

Being able to mix with other children outside the family is only part of the issue of socialisation. People wonder how home-educated children will manage to function normally in society without going through the process which everyone else has had to go through. The fact that this process is often perceived to be unpleasant may add to its importance for some: school is sometimes seen as a preparation for the harsh realities of life. And life – like school – is often seen as a place where you have to work hard and where you cannot do what you want to do. It seems to be this aspect of home education which particularly bothers some people: home-educated children often learn quickly without a lot of hard grind and they clearly enjoy themselves along the way. Many parents who have chosen the 'otherwise' have done so precisely for this reason. They feel that there is plenty of time later to get to grips with the grim realities of boring, repetitive jobs. Indeed, they may choose home education because they do not want their children to accept such limitations. They may hope instead to foster resourcefulness and individuality which will prepare them for more adventurous, interesting lives.

Summary

In summary, parents who choose to keep full responsibility for their children's education do so for a wide variety of reasons. It is particularly difficult to give a profile of a typical parent who chooses home education. Both ends of the political spectrum are here. The approach may be highly structured or it may be a rejection of formal aspects of schooling. The decision to educate children at home may stem from the parents' beliefs or from the needs and abilities of the children themselves. Looking back at home education in the past, there were always theorists (Rousseau, 1966) and practical activists (Cobbett, 1930). There were those who imposed rigorous training schedules on their offspring from their earliest years: J S Mill was one of the better-known products of such a programme. There were others who were comparatively neglectful about their children's education, as the childhood accounts of a number of home-educated women writers have testified. It is likely there will continue to be those who aim for high attainments and those who are content to let their children learn as they play.

Contact Addresses

For information on Education Otherwise, send a stamped addressed envelope to:

Education Otherwise
PO Box 120
Leamington Spa
Warwickshire
CV32 7ER

Recorded message of area telephone numbers on: 0926 886828

Growing Without Schooling
Holt Associates
2269 Mass Ave
Cambridge
MA 02140
USA.

World-Wide Education Service
Strode House
44–50 Osnaburgh Street
London NW1 3NN

References

Baker, J (1964) *Children in Chancery* London, Hutchinson.
Bendell, J (1987) *School's Out: Educating your Child at Home* Bath, Ashgrove Press.
Boyd, D (1973) *Elites and their Education* Windsor, NFER.
Cobbett, W (1930 [1830]) *Advice to Young Men and (Incidentally) Young Women* London, The Curwen Press.
Deakin, M (1972) *The Children on the Hill* London, André Deutsch.
Department of Education and Science (1991) *The Parents' Charter* London, DES.
Deutsch, D and Wolf, K (1991) *Home Education and the Law* (2nd edn) Oxford, Deutsch and Wolf.
Dore, R (1976) *The Diploma Disease* London, Allen & Unwin.
Douglas, J W B (1964) *The Home and the School: A Study of Ability and Attainment in the Primary School* London, MacGibbon & Kee.
Griggs, C (1985) *Private Education in Britain* Lewes, Falmer Press.
Holt, J (1981) *Teach Your Own* Brightlingsea, Lighthouse Books.
Illich, I (1971) *Deschooling Society* London, Calder & Boyars.
Rosenthal, R and Jacobson, L (1968) *Pygmalion in the Classroom: Teacher Expectation and Pupils' Intellectual Development* New York, Holt, Rinehart & Winston.
Robbins, L R (1963) *Higher Education: Report of the Committee* London, HMSO.
Rousseau, J-J (1966 [1762]) *Emile* London, Dent.

Chapter 12

Racism, Parental Choice and the Law

Peter Cumper

Modern Britain has plenty of room for diversity and variety. But there cannot be room for separation or segregation.

John Patten, 1989

In 1987 a group of white Dewsbury parents refused to enrol their children in a school where 85 per cent of pupils were Asian. The parents had requested that their children attend two overwhelmingly 'white' schools. However, Kirklees Education Authority insisted that the preferred schools were oversubscribed, and allocated the children to the mainly Asian Headfield Middle School. Incensed by this, the parents boycotted Headfield and for a year 26 white children were educated in a makeshift school above a pub. The parents took their case to the High Court and were successful. Kirklees Council agreed to meet the parents' demands and conceded that it had failed to publish its admissions quota, as required by Section 8 of the Education Act 1980. Thus the parents' ultimate victory was based not on the substantive principle of parental choice but on a procedural irregularity.

In the aftermath of the court proceedings, the Dewsbury parents issued a statement stressing that they were 'deeply hurt by the suggestions that they had been racially motivated' (Bradney, 1989, p 52). They insisted that they had merely wanted their children to receive a traditional British Christian education; thus their preference had been based on *cultural*, not *racial* grounds. Such subtle distinctions were evidently lost on sections of the press. The *Daily Mail* categorically asserted: 'whatever the legal niceties and whatever the avowals and denials, this fight has been about two things: choice and race' (13 July 1988). *The Independent* considered that the 'Dewsbury dispute has forced on the agenda some awkward issues about the implications of all-Asian, all-white, or all-black schools' (10 September 1987). Clearly, the Commission for Racial Equality (CRE) shared these sentiments. In its annual report, the CRE expressed concern that 'more scope for parental choice might result in racial segregation', and lead to a recurrence of the Dewsbury affair (CRE, 1987). But should the courts intervene if parents wish to enrol a child in a school on cultural or racial grounds? The fact that Kirklees Borough Council chose to settle, giving the parents a 'technical' victory, released the High Court from having to answer such a question. However, in the more recent Cleveland case, British judges went some way towards addressing this issue.

The Cleveland Case

In November 1987, Mrs Jenny Carney sent a letter to her Local Education Authority (LEA), Cleveland County Council. She requested that her five-year-old daughter Katrice be transferred from Abingdon Road Infants' School in Middlesbrough (where 60 per cent of pupils are Asian), to the nearby Martin Grove School (where 98 per cent of pupils are white). Mrs Carney wrote:

> I don't think it's fair for Katrice to go through school with about four white friends and the rest Pakistani, which she does not associate with. I think the school [Abingdon Road] is a very good school, but I don't think it's right when she comes home singing in Pakistani ... I just don't want her to learn this language ... I just want her to go to a school where there will be in the majority white children, not Pakistani.

The headteacher of Abingdon Road School unsuccessfully tried to dissuade Mrs Carney, and Cleveland Education Authority, acting on legal advice, reluctantly authorised Katrice's move to the new school. The Authority felt that since its duty under Section 6 of the Education Act 1980 to comply with the wishes of Mrs Carney overrode the provisions of the Race Relations Act 1976, it had no option but to transfer Katrice Carney to the new school. Cleveland Education Authority, unhappy that Mrs Carney's request had forced them into an act of racial segregation, then contacted the CRE. Ironically it was the

CRE which sought a declaration that Cleveland County Council itself had committed an act of discrimination contrary to the Race Relations Act 1976. This imposes a duty on a local education authority not to perform any act which constitutes racial discrimination. Thus the main arguments put forward by the CRE were that:

- Mrs Carney's request had been made on 'racial' grounds;
- the transfer constituted an act of racial 'segregation' under Section 1(2) of the Race Relations Act 1976;
- Cleveland County Council's legal duty to comply with Mrs Carney's preference (Section 6 of the Education 1980), was qualified by a duty on local education authorities not to discriminate (Section 18 Race Relations Act 1976).

These submissions were rejected in the High Court (Macpherson J) and the Court of Appeal (Parker LJ). Both Macpherson J and Parker LJ exonerated Mrs Carney of charges of racism, stressing that her motives were *cultural* not *racial.* Nevertheless, according to Macpherson J, it was the CRE's third argument, the relationship between Section 18 of the 1976 Act and Section 6 of the 1980 Act, which was the 'crucial issue in this case'. Section 6 of the Education Act 1980 puts LEAs under a duty to comply with a parent's preference for a particular school. Section 18 of the Race Relations Act makes it 'unlawful for an LEA in carrying out any of its functions under the Education Acts to do any act which constitutes racial discrimination.' But Section 41 of the Race Relations Act qualifies this by providing that 'nothing in Parts II to IV [of the Act] shall render unlawful any act of discrimination done in pursuance of any enactment.'

The CRE's argument that the Section 6 duty to comply with parental preference was governed or overridden by the Race Relations Act was rejected by Macpherson J. He held that apart from an exception in Section 6(3) (which was not relevant in this case), an LEA has no right to reject a parent's request for a transfer on the ground that it disapproves of the reasons for the move: 'the parent is not obliged to be logical or even reasonable in his or her decision to ask for a move ... the parent's reasons are irrelevant.' Thus Macpherson J concluded that it was Parliament's intention that parental preference should be 'supreme' in this area.

In giving the sole judgment in the Court of Appeal, Parker LJ agreed that Parliament had not intended Section 6 of the 1980 Act to be governed by the Race Relations Act. Such an argument was 'somewhat bizarre' and was 'positively inimical' to the purposes of the 1980 Education Act. Unfortunately Parker LJ failed to issue guidelines or directly tackle the thorny question of balancing parental preference (Section 6) with the duty not to discriminate (Section 18 of the 1976 Act). His way round this quandary was to refer to Section 41 of the Race Relations Act 1976, which prevents decisions authorised by another statute, from being prohibited as racially discriminatory. Thus the mandatory duty under Section 6 of the 1980 Act could ultimately be saved by Section 41 of the Race Relations Act 1976. In coming to this conclusion, Parker LJ implicitly endorsed Macpherson J's earlier recognition of the supremacy of parental preference.

In the aftermath of the Cleveland case, the press portrayed the decision simply as a victory for parental choice. Headlines such as 'Race: every parent's right to choose' (*Evening Standard*, 18 October 1991), 'Judge places school right above race law' (*The Guardian*, 19 October 1991) and 'Racist motives no bar to parents' choice of school' (*The Independent*, 19 October 1991), obscured the reality that on the facts of the case, the perceived conflict between the Race Relations Act and the Education Act did not actually arise. This was because both Macpherson J and Parker LJ rejected the CRE's argument that the child's transfer to a school with a tiny proportion of Asians, (2 per cent as against 60 per cent), could constitute 'segregation'. In the High Court, Macpherson J stated that 'segregation' means 'the keeping apart of racial groups'. Since Katrice Carney could still meet Asians in her new school, it was a misuse of language to describe her transfer to the new school as an act of segregation. Parker LJ reached a similar conclusion that there could be no racial segregation 'on any ordinary use of language'. On these facts there was no conflict. But what *should* be the relationship between the Race Relations Act and the principle of parental choice under the Education Act 1980? Mrs Carney was able to leave court, in Macpherson J's words, without any 'racist stain'. But what of the parent who wishes to transfer a child for reasons which are unambiguously racist? Even the Secretary of the Parental Alliance for Choice in Education, the pressure group which supported Mrs Carney, warned in the aftermath of the case: 'the biggest problem ... will be how to discourage parents from wanting to move their children for purely racist reasons' (*Times Educational Supplement*, 8 November 1991). Could the Cleveland case create a flood of applications from parents wishing to transfer their children to new schools on racial grounds?

Floodgate Fears

Such fears were expressed in the wake of Macpherson J's ruling. Apart from the predictably sensationalist reaction of the tabloid press, *The Daily Telegraph* warned that LEAs could face an 'avalanche of applications from parents to move their children to schools with a different racial mix' (19 October 1991), while *The Times* noted that the ruling had 'potentially serious implications for multi-racial education' (19 October 1991). Mindful of this, the Chairman of the Cleveland Education Committee expressed little joy at his Council's High Court victory. Instead he lamented the decision which he felt heralded a 'black day for education in a multi-racial society' (*Newsnight*, 18 October 1991). His pessimism was shared by the CRE. In its Annual Report it warned of the 'potentially serious consequences' of the Cleveland case, and suggested that it could have 'significant effects within the school system', by encouraging a 'trend towards segregation' (CRE, 1991, p 16).

Macpherson J dismissed 'floodgate' fears as 'exaggerated' and was 'confident' that racial prejudice would not motivate parents to transfer their children to new schools. But less than a month after his judgment, it was reported that white parents in Tower Hamlets, East London, were refusing to send their 12-year-old daughter to a school where almost 80 per cent of pupils were Bengali. The child's mother, echoing the words of Mrs Carney, defended her actions by claiming: 'I am not a racist, but most of the children at St Paul's Way [the school in question] are Asian. Most of them speak English badly and they will hold her back' (*Times Educational Supplement*, 15 November 1991). Is this just an isolated incident, or could it be a first step in the creation of racially homogeneous schools? It seems that it is not only white parents who are requesting transfers. In Cleveland, shortly after the Carney case, a Libyan Muslim successfully requested that his son be transferred from a mainly white school, to one with a more equal racial mix (*The Sun*, 30 April 1989). Could it be that as a result of the Carney case, the ghost of racial segregation will soon be stalking the corridors of British schools? In the short term this is unlikely. LEAs contacted after the Cleveland case did not anticipate any rush of transfers (*The Times Educational Supplement*, 25 October 1991). But what in the long run?

A Harris opinion poll in 1987 found that 40 per cent of white parents would rather have their children educated with their own ethnic group, as compared to 15 per cent of black and 19 per cent of Asian parents (Jones, 1989). Of course, there is a major difference between responding to a questionnaire in which one stipulates a preference for schools based on race, and actually moving a child to a new school on such grounds. Yet what if race relations rapidly deteriorate in the future? Is it not likely that, in such circumstances, irrational xenophobic fears may manifest themselves in school transfers?

The Cleveland case means that 'the door is now undoubtedly open to parents to use the right of choice ... in a racist manner' (Harris, 1992). It is an unpleasant scenario, but in the long term, might the trickle of parents requesting racial transfers become a 'tide' or even a 'flood'? Parker LJ failed to discuss the wider implications of his judgment, while Macpherson J twice stressed that such cases are rare. However, he added that should his judgment precipitate a rush of similar applications, 'Parliament would quickly react'. In spite of this there have already been calls for the introduction of legislation which would prohibit transfer requests on racial grounds. The Association of Metropolitan Authorities has argued that fresh legislation could spare local authorities from having to comply with racially motivated school transfers, which might undermine their own equal opportunities policies (*The Daily Telegraph*, 19 October 1991). Similar calls for legal reform have been made by the Deputy County Secretary of Cleveland County Council (ibid) and by the CRE (Coussins, 1991).

But if legislation outlawing school transfers on racial grounds is to be introduced, there will inevitably be problems defining *racist* transfers. Would parents who object to *multi-cultural* education be covered? And what of parents who request a transfer because their children are learning about minority religious faiths and celebrating their festivals? Or parents who for *educational reasons only* want their children to study with those whose mother tongue is English? Are cultural prejudices synonymous with racial bias? Distinctions between race and culture are not easy to draw. One view sees *race* defined biologically as primarily the colour of one's skin, with the key elements of a *culture* as language, religion, morals and political and economic organisation (Naylor, 1989, p 136). These theories, concentrating on the separation of 'race' and 'culture', have been condemned as the 'new racism' (Troyna and Carrington, 1990). It has been submitted that 'the new racism elevates "British Culture" into a superior way of life, seeing it as under threat from "other", "alien" and implicitly inferior cultures' (Vincent, 1992). In rejecting the notion that all cultures are inherently equal, it argues that cultural relativism 'inevitably signifies moral relativism and a loss of all sense of direction' (Naylor, 1989). Not surprisingly, such a view has been endorsed mainly by those on the political right.

If Parliament effects legislation prohibiting racial transfers, the courts will have to decide whether *culturally* motivated transfers are legitimate or are merely a smokescreen for racism. Yet even if the courts manage to differentiate between 'race' and 'culture', a second problem remains: the *implementation* of legislation which prohibits the transfer of children on racial grounds? Could well-educated parents articulate racial prejudice in oblique terms, so as to fall outside the scope of the Act? Would the onus be on parents to prove that a transfer was *not* racially motivated? Might local authorities and the courts become the 'thought police' of education? This scenario seems particularly undesirable. For some it may resemble the Orwellian nightmare of the state peering into the minds of individuals. Such disquiet probably contributed to an editorial in *The Independent* (24 April 1990) which concluded:

> On balance the drawbacks of letting officials dictate to parents where they can send their children are worse than the admittedly alarming risk that British schools will become more divided.

Macpherson J was aware of the practical difficulties any scrutiny of parents' motives would incur. He described the burden which would be placed on LEAs as 'intolerable', and pointed out that such a policy would mean that a parent expressing 'some mildly objectionable reason', could be penalised, unlike a 'grossly racialist parent' who remained silent. Thus such legislation could be counter-productive, unfairly stigmatising honest, ill-educated parents, while failing to catch cunning covert racists. The CRE will undoubtedly disagree. In a tersely worded press release following the Court of Appeal decision, the Commission reaffirmed its concern that 'parental choice under education law is not covered by the Race Relations Act' (31 July 1992).

The government's response to the Cleveland decision was rather different. Education Minister Michael Fallon openly expressed his satisfaction at the ruling and concluded: 'it is a victory for the right of parental choice *over all others'* (*The Sunday Times*, 20 October 1991, my emphasis). This reaction is not surprising. The government has long been committed to what has been described as 'the individualist rights approach': the view that stress should be placed on 'the individual parents' school requests without regard for general policy concerns' (Tweedie, 1986). Yet if parental choice is 'supreme' in the field of school transfers, should it not be so in other areas of education? What of the campaign by minority faith groups to establish their own state-funded schools? Many of these parents are of Asian origin. To what extent have they enjoyed the benefits of increased parent power?

Choice and Minority Groups

In the UK today there are about 1 million Muslims, 500,000 Sikhs, and 300,000 Hindus (Central Office of Information, 1992). There have been numerous attempts within these groups to set up their own schools. Britain's Muslims have been particularly vigorous in this campaign. Twenty-eight Muslim schools have been established, though as yet none has received any financial support from the state. A handful of Sikh, Hindu, Orthodox Jewish and Seventh Day Adventist schools also remain privately funded. Nevertheless there are 4,600 voluntary aided (state funded) church schools in Britain, and 98 per cent of these schools are controlled by the Anglican and Roman Catholic churches. Such an anomaly is difficult to justify. Jack Straw, the former Labour Shadow Education spokesman, has argued that 'in equity', major world faiths with followers in the UK should be entitled to establish their own state-sponsored religious schools (Straw, 1989). In practice this is yet to happen. So far Muslim requests for voluntary-aided status have been rejected on the basis that there is a surplus of places in neighbouring schools. This is in accordance with the principle that new state-funded schools may not be established in areas where existing schools already have vacancies. With many Asians living in inner-city areas where schools often have surplus places, Jack Straw has claimed that this policy unfairly discriminates against Muslims (*Times Educational Supplement*, 31 January 1991).

The most widely publicised attempt by Muslims to obtain voluntary-aided status has been in the London Borough of Brent. There the Islamia Primary School was refused voluntary-aided status in 1990 on the ground that there were already vacant places in neighbouring schools, a decision confirmed by the Secretary of State for Education in August 1993. Some may consider that the 'spirit' of the Cleveland case adds weight to the argument that the aspirations of the Muslim parents should outweigh the policy of the Department for Education (DfE) not to establish a new school where existing schools in an area have vacancies. But as a matter of law, such a view is naive and simplistic. Legally the two cases can be easily distinguished. For example, the Cleveland case involves the *transfer* of existing pupils at a school, while the Brent case relates to the *establishment* of a new school. Be this as it may, such legal distinctions are unlikely to comfort a Muslim community frustrated by their lack of success in campaigning for voluntary-aided schools.

In January 1992, the Muslim newsletter *Islamia* reported the Cleveland case as a decision which 'reinforces the principle of parental choice but also underlines the fact that some parents are more equal than others' (*Islamia*, 17, p 7). In fact, there is a widespread sense of injustice felt by many Asian Muslim parents and leaders. Kalam Siddiqui, Director of the Muslim Institute and founder of the Muslim Parliament, has complained: 'There are Catholic, Church of England and Jewish Schools, but we have repeatedly been refused aid. On this issue, we are just about reaching the end of our tether' (*The Times*, 6 January 1992).

These sentiments are shared by Dr Azam Baig, the principal of the Islamia Primary School. In an oblique reference to the Government's education White Paper, Dr Baig asks: 'What does choice and diversity mean if some parents are not allowed a choice?' (*The Guardian*, 23 March 1993). Yet for Muslim educationalists, the future is not entirely bleak; as a result of recent educational reforms, Muslims now have another option: grant maintained status.

Under the Education Reform Act 1988 all LEA-maintained primary, middle and secondary schools are eligible to apply for grant maintained status (GMS). If the parents at a school vote for GMS in a ballot, the school's governors must publish proposals explaining how a new governing body would run a grant maintained school. The proposals form the basis of the application to the Secretary of State for Education, who decides each application on its merits. If the Secretary of State is satisfied that the school has a viable future, it may 'opt out' of LEA control and manage its own finances under direct funding from central government.

The financial rewards associated with grant maintained status are considerable. For the year 1993–94, the 337 schools which have so far opted out of LEA control, will receive capital grants totalling £77 million, the equivalent of nearly 13 per cent of the total grant for the 24,000 schools in England and Wales (*The Guardian*, 26 January 1993, p 12). It has been estimated that by 1996, 'most' maintained secondary schools, and a significant proportion of all state primary schools, could be grant maintained (DfE, 1992, p 1). Some Muslim leaders have therefore suggested that Muslim governors in predominantly Asian schools should exert control by opting into the grant maintained system, where LEAs are unresponsive to Muslim grievances (Mabud, 1992). Others have argued that grant maintained status offers an opportunity for Muslim self-determination in education, with the possibility of 'opting into Islam' (Yaseen, 1991).

Thus, it is reasonable to conclude that in the long term, GMS 'may offer an attractive alternative' for groups such as Muslims, 'which have been attempting for years without success to establish schools with voluntary aided status' (Meredith, 1992). The social consequences of this are unclear. Of course, Muslims are not a race and it is dangerous to confuse ethnicity with religious belief. Yet the Commission for Racial Equality has suggested that the demand for minority faith schools is to be understood as a response to racism in British society (CRE, 1990). This link between race and religion is illustrated by the fact that the majority of British Muslims are of Asian origin, so is there a danger that predominantly Muslim schools which opt out of LEA control, may be seen as 'black' schools?

Grant Maintained Schools and Race

The idea of creating schools which might cater almost exclusively for people of one colour and culture, has traditionally been received with caution. In 1983, Bradford County Council refused an application for five voluntary-aided schools from the Muslim Parents Association. In its report, Bradford Council noted how education can promote understanding and reconciliation. However, it pointed out that education can be a 'more powerful tool for promoting division', and that in Bradford divisions would be exacerbated not only by religion, but by colour: 'Muslim schools would risk becoming black schools and encouraging racial prejudice' (Bradford Metropolitan District Council, 1983). More recently it has been claimed that state-funded Muslim schools would be ethnically divisive (Hutchings, 1993). Could a similar charge be levelled at predominantly Muslim schools which seek greater autonomy by opting for grant maintained status?

The divisiveness charge is difficult to substantiate. Yet there is a real danger that grant maintained schools, with a majority of Asian or Muslim pupils and governors, could be *perceived* as *black* schools. It is possible that some white parents may be influenced by such factors, in refraining from sending their children to these schools. After all the *white flight* from multiracial inner-city areas, is not a completely unknown phenomenon. It particularly explains the official figures which reveal that there are 12 state schools where the pupils are 100 per cent of ethnic minority origin, 50 where the figure is 90 per cent or more and 230 where 75 per cent of children were born of ethnic minority parents (*The Independent*, 15 January 1988). The possibility of even further racial segregation is obviously an undesirable consequence of grant maintained status.

However, it seems likely that race may also become an emotive factor in the *management* of opted-out schools: witness the scenario at Stratford School in East London in 1991–92. In this case two governors, Mr Ghulam Shaida and Mr Harbhajan Singh, accused the white headteacher, Mrs Anne Snelling, of racism. The governors were particularly incensed by Mrs Snelling's appointment of mainly white staff, in a grant maintained school where most of the pupils were of Asian origin. Mr Shaida criticised the staffing policy by claiming that the school was in danger of 'becoming like South Africa, where a handful rule the majority' (*The Times*, 24 January 1992). In a bizarre series of events, Harbhajan Singh allegedly called the headteacher a racist and a liar during school assembly. He was immediately suspended but was reinstated by the other governors. Mrs Snelling was then herself suspended, only to be reinstated after the intervention of the Secretary of State for Education. Around the same time, the two dissident governors sought to address the school assembly against the wishes of the headteacher. The police were called and Mrs Snelling was accused of assaulting Mr Shaida, while she replied by naming Mr Shaida in a writ for slander.

Essentially the row at Stratford School focused on the balance of power between the governors of a grant maintained school and its headteacher. The governing body, which must include five parents and one elected teacher, is the employer of the staff. Under Section 57(3) of the Education Reform Act 1988, governors have the power to 'do anything which appears to them to be necessary or expedient for the purpose of the school'. Guidelines issued by the Department for Education stress that governors may set 'the strategic framework' for a school; that they may formulate policies, but may not personally implement them (Department of Education and Science, 1992). This is the function of the headteacher, who with other staff is responsible for the everyday running of the school. Thus 'governance of a school is an overseeing role, not a hands-on managing role' (ibid, 1992).

In *theory* this seems clear; but in *practice*, the potential for conflict between power-hungry governors and an autonomous headteacher seems considerable. When the conflict arose at Stratford School, bitterness was intensified by charges of racism. The Asian protagonists clearly saw the conflict in racial terms and they were supported by the London Collective of Black Governors (LCBG). The Chairman of the LCBG, Muhammed Haque, stressed that 'the whole battle is about racism' (*The Times*, 24 January 1992), and claimed that 'whenever African and Asian governors have attempted to do their job and to try to run the schools in the best way, both local authorities and central government have stepped in to defy the governors' authority' (*The Times Educational Supplement*, 21 March 1992).

The row at Stratford School fizzled out with Mr Shaida and Mr Singh opting to boycott the school's governing body. But what of the future? Might there be another Stratford? There it was alleged that Mr Shaida sought to play on the fears of Asian parents by claiming that their children were in 'moral danger', because of the headteacher's liberal policies (*The Observer*, 1 March 1992). What if the Muslim governors of a grant maintained school seek to protect their daughters by requiring that all Muslim girls must keep their heads covered? And at Stratford School, the appointment of staff was an acrimonious issue. What if some Muslim governors insist that the appointment of teachers must satisfy certain criteria?

An editorial in the *Muslim Educational Quarterly* suggested that anyone who is 'an atheist or non-believer will not be appointed or retained' in the service of a predominantly Muslim school which has opted out (Ashraf, 1988). The implications of such a policy are unclear. Does it mean that headteachers, teachers, secretaries, canteen staff and even caretakers in Muslim dominated schools which opt out, will be forced to resign? Would Muslim governors be prepared to appoint homosexual or single-parent teachers? The educational aspirations of Muslim parents have for too long been ignored by the British educational establishment. In view of this, is it possible that some Muslim governors may try to 'Islamise' a mainly Muslim school which opts out of LEA control? While the chances of this happening are remote, it cannot be entirely discounted. After all, who could have predicted the farcical events at Stratford School? Muslim values are very different from those accepted by secular Western liberal society. Thus there is a danger that any conflict will be portrayed in *racial*, not *religious* terms. Even John Patten inadvertently blurred this distinction when he referred to 'all *ethnic* minority groups, including Muslims' (1989).

Ironically, it is John Patten, as the present Secretary of State for Education, who may have to intervene if minority faith governors risk turning grant maintained schools into denominational schools. Yet it is a grave error to focus only on the racial implications of giving power to minority faith parents. Mr Patten will also have to ensure that white parents at grant maintained schools do not adopt admissions policies which unfairly penalise black applicants. Criteria such as 'the sibling rule', whereby priority for places goes to children with brothers and sisters already at the preferred school, may lead to the exclusion of black children. There is a risk that some white parents may try and abuse grant maintained status, in order to create 'white fortresses'. The Commission for Racial Equality has recognised this (Haviland, 1988, p 118), as has the National Union of Teachers (ibid., p 130). Of course the Department for Education has wide powers of intervention should it transpire that a school's admissions policy is racist. But the practical problems of detecting illegal admissions policies must not be overlooked. For example, in 1992, when the CRE found that the admissions criteria of two Watford grammar schools unfairly disadvantaged Asian applicants, the CRE accepted that the 'sibling rule' was lawful (as a result of its educational advantages), even though it was 'discriminatory in its impact' (CRE, 1992). As a result of such factors, it has been claimed that grant maintained status will 'segregate further black children into schools with falling rolls and low staff morale' and that 'the parents who will receive the greatest support in their demands for choice will be white parents' (Flude and Hammer, 1990, p 179).

Conclusion

Has the government really considered the implications of granting parents unfettered choice? In 1987, its spokesperson Baroness Hooper insisted: 'if we are offering freedom of choice to parents, we must allow that choice to operate. If it ends up with a segregated system, then so be it' (*Times Educational Supplement*, 4 December 1987). In the absence of any condemnation of these remarks by successive Education Secretaries, one is left with the impression that silence denotes consent. Thus it has been argued that 'this Ministerial refusal to accept liability for any adverse consequences arising from the operation of the free market leaves the government open to the charge of "discrimination by proxy"' (Vincent, 1992). Inevitably demographical factors may mean that schools have a disproportionate racial mix. But is it proper that the government's educational reforms could exacerbate rather than ameliorate, racial polarisation in the classroom?

In the House of Lords during a recent debate on the funding of minority faith schools, Baroness Flather observed that 'parental choice cannot be paramount. It must be balanced with the needs of society and those of the real consumers, the children themselves' (*Hansard*, vol 526, no 52, 4 March 1991). So what of children's rights? Are they necessarily synonymous with those of their parents? Can it be in the interests of children if schools are created which crystallise those racial, cultural and religious issues that separate ethnic minority pupils from their white counterparts? If we fail to take cognisance of the racial implications of educational consumerism, do we not risk doing a great disservice to the schoolchildren of tomorrow? As George Orwell wrote: 'if liberty means anything at all it means the right to tell people what they do not want to hear' (Orwell, 1945). Parental choice is an important human right. But should it be absolute? The time is right for a serious debate on whether and to what extent parents' rights should be curtailed by the interests of the child or the collective good.

References

Ashraf, S A (1988) 'Editorial' *Muslim Educational Quarterly*, 5, 3.

Bradford Metropolitan District Council (1983) *Report on the Muslim Parents Association's Proposals for Muslim Voluntary Aided Schools* unpublished.

Bradney, A (1989) 'The Dewsbury Affair and the Education Reform Act 1988' *Education and the Law*, 1, 2, pp 51–57.

Central Office of Information (1992) *Britain 1992 – An Official Handbook* London, HMSO.

Coussins, J (1991) 'Clarify the Cleveland law' *Times Educational Supplement*, 8 November.

Commission for Racial Equality (1987) *Annual Report* London, CRE.

Commission for Racial Equality (1990) *Schools of Faith: Religious Schools in a Multi-cultural Society* London, CRE.

Commission for Racial Equality (1991) *Annual Report* London, CRE.

Commission for Racial Equality (1992) *Secondary School Admissions. Report of a Formal Investigation Into Hertfordshire County Council* London, CRE.

Department for Education (1992) *Grant Maintained Schools: Questions Parents Ask* London, DfE.

Department of Education and Science (1992) *The Role and Function of Governing Bodies of Grant Maintained Schools* London, DES.

Flude, M and Hammer, M (1990) *The Education Reform Act 1988* London, Falmer Press.

Harris, N (1992) 'Educational choice in a multi-cultural society' *Public Law*, Winter, pp 522–33.

Haviland, J (ed) (1988) *Take Care, Mr Baker* London, Fourth Estate.

Hutchings, J (1993) 'Don't fund apartheid' *The Times* 15 February.

Jones, K (1989) *Right Turn* London, Hutchinson.

Mabud, S A (1992), 'A Muslim response to the Education Reform Act 1988' *British Journal of Religious Education*, 14, 2, pp 88–98.

Meredith, P (1992) 'Opting out litigation: the Newham experience' *Education and the Law*, 4, 2, pp 69–74.

Naylor, F (1989) *Dewsbury: The School Above the Pub* London, Claridge Press.

Orwell, G (1945) Preface to *Animal Farm* London, Penguin.

Patten, J (1989) Letter to Mr Iqbal Sacranie, cited in *Muslims and the Law in Multi-Faith Britain: The Need for Reform*, memorandum submitted by the UK Action Committee on Islamic Affairs to the Rt Hon Michael Howard, MP, 29 July 1993.

Straw, J (1989) 'Islam, women and Muslim schools' *Muslim Education Quarterly*, 6, 4, pp 7–9.

Troyna, B and Carrington, B (1990) *Education, Racism and Reform* London, Routledge.

Tweedie, J (1986) 'Rights in social programmes: the case of parental choice of the school' *Public Law*, Autumn, pp 407–436.

Vincent, C (1992) 'Tolerating intolerance? Parental choice and race relations – the Cleveland case' *Journal of Education Policy*, 7, 5, pp 429–445.

Yaseen, M (1991), 'Trigger for change' *Managing Schools Today*, 1, 4, pp 32–33.

Chapter 13

PACE in Action: Some Case Studies from the Parental Alliance for Choice in Education

Fred Naylor

It would be going too far to maintain that parental choice has become a new organising principle in English education. It is, however, a term that is being heard more and more. And as the main political parties come to grips with its potentialities they are being forced to give it more serious attention. Given the potential conflict between liberty and equality and the swing of the pendulum towards egalitarianism in the 1960s and 1970s, no one should underestimate the difficulties in restoring the balance by a re-emphasis on individual freedom. Nothing marks the rise of the egalitarian tide better than the change in attitudes to mixed ability teaching over a five-year period at the end of the 1960s. In 1964, Jackson was pleading for an experimental branch, responsible to the Ministry, which would set up primary schools in which mixed-ability classes could be established (1964, p 132). In 1969, the Schools Council's Second Sixth Form Working Party, in the run-up to the 'Q' and 'F' proposals, was being pressed hard to extend mixed ability teaching into sixth forms.

The Parental Alliance for Choice in Education (PACE) was set up in 1985. The inaugural meeting, under the Chairmanship of Baroness Cox, had an accidental element which was to prove significant for the future of PACE. The original intention had been to bring together under one banner a number of local groups, from as far apart as York and Salisbury, fighting to save their grammar schools. An uninvited guest from Merrywood Boys' School, Bristol – an 11–18 comprehensive which was threatened with closure by Avon Council – was disconcerted to discover the preoccupation with grammar schools. He was quickly assured that the concern for parental choice was not confined to such schools. This enabled PACE to clarify its aims at the outset.

The principle which would underlie its work was Article 2 of Protocol No 1 of the European Convention on Human Rights. This gives parents the right to 'education and teaching in conformity with their own religious and philosophical convictions'. This even-handedness has proved its greatest strength. It extends beyond support for the different philosophies represented by comprehensive and selective schooling. And it is now a matter of history that the PACE campaign to save Merrywood Boys' School was the first in a series which ended in successful court action.

The support to parents given by PACE since its inception in 1985 falls into three main categories:
- the court cases (and potential court cases) arising out of unsuccessful complaints to the Secretary of State;
- help with school admission appeals;
- general help to those who find themselves at a loss when dealing with remote bureaucrats handsomely primed with public funds.

The last of these is too extensive and diverse to describe here, but the work of PACE in the two other areas will be outlined. The issues raised will then be dealt with more fully.

Court Cases

Not all the court cases will be described here. For example, the Cleveland case (see Chapter 12) did not involve PACE, but its Honorary Secretary (Fred Naylor) and solicitor (Roger Peach) both acted in an individual capacity for Jenny Carney, and were responsible for securing her representation in court and subsequent clearance of any charge of racism. All the parties in the case – the Commission for Racial Equality (CRE), Cleveland Council and the Department of Education and Science – had been prepared to stereotype her as a racist.

The Merrywood case

The Merrywood case had a number of interesting features, not least of which was its knock-on effect in other areas. PACE's initial advice to the

Merrywood parents was to seek a judicial review of Avon's decision to close the school, a decision which had been approved by the Secretary of State, Sir Keith Joseph. It seemed a good test case for establishing the right of parents to single-sex education on philosophical grounds. The parents were enthusiastic but their counsel, Mr David Pannick, advised that they would stand a better chance of success on 'equal opportunities' grounds. Avon wished to solve its problem of small sixth forms in this part of Bristol by stripping a number of schools of their sixth forms and creating a sixth form college on the Merrywood Boys' site. They had no plans to close the corresponding Merrywood Girls' School, mainly in recognition of the demand for single-sex schooling by the Asians in the area. It was Avon's failure to treat boys and girls equally that Mr Pannick chose to attack. Sir Keith Joseph, at the prospect of court action, decided that he had misdirected himself, and withdrew his approval of the proposed closure. Avon, however, resolved to defend its action in the court. Mr Pannick's subsequent victory was the first application of the Sex Discrimination Act to schooling in the UK.

PACE gave free educational and legal advice to the Merrywood parents on how to proceed. The parents were successful in obtaining legal aid, but were required to contribute to the initial costs. This is PACE's normal method of working.

The outcome was that the parents achieved their goal, but the parental right to single-sex education had nonetheless not been established in law. If Avon had decided to close down the girls' school simultaneously the case would necessarily have been fought on the issue of parental choice. It must, however, be said that it is doubtful whether the law is sufficiently robust for this. As it was, the Merrywood decision encouraged the Equal Opportunities Commission to mount a successful challenge to the practice in the City of Birmingham of providing more grammar school places for boys than for girls. The City Council took the case to the House of Lords before conceding defeat. Despite this legal ruling, however, the situation in Birmingham has not yet been resolved. The Merrywood case has been quoted in other court actions and has played an important part in decisions on school provision in other authorities.

The Dewsbury case

Kirklees Metropolitan Council in 1987 refused 26 Dewsbury children admission to the schools of their parents' choice, even though there were enough places available and parents from the same district had been allowed to send their children to these schools before 1987. Instead, Kirklees – in pursuit of its policy on multicultural education – expected them to go to a school where the population was overwhelmingly Asian (and which ironically was a Church of England voluntary controlled school).

The strength of the parents' feeling was such that they decided to challenge the authority. In a highly effective campaign, which captured the attention of the nation's press and TV for a whole year, they withdrew their children to a room over a pub and with the help of volunteer teachers transformed this room into an efficient and popular school. Advised by PACE, the parents prepared their case for court. The judicial review of Kirklees' decisions was heard in the High Court in London in July 1988. On the second day, Kirklees dramatically threw in its hand and granted the parents admission for their children to the schools of their choice. The court was not called upon to pronounce on the Council's multicultural policy, which the parents claimed was preventing their children from being 'educated in a traditional English and Christian environment' (Naylor, 1989, p 154). The Council agreed that it was this policy – designed 'to counter a Eurocentric syllabus' – that lay at the heart of the case.

The Cardinal Vaughan case

Concurrent with the Dewsbury case, PACE advised the parents of Cardinal Vaughan School, in the Roman Catholic Diocese of Westminster, in their successful High Court action to restrain the Trustee, Cardinal Hume, from summarily dismissing those school governors who would not agree to the school's loss of its successful sixth form. This had echoes of the Merrywood case. One of the effects of secondary organisation along comprehensive lines was the production of non-viable sixth forms (Naylor, 1981). The reaction of many authorities was to strip a number of schools like Cardinal Vaughan of their sixth forms while concentrating their pupils in a newly established sixth form college. Planners expected to be allowed to dig another hole to extricate themselves from the one they had created by ignoring parental choice in the first place.

The Manchester and Ealing cases (and others involving multi-faith worship)

Both the Manchester and Ealing cases came under the new complaints procedure introduced in the Education Reform Act (ERA) 1988. In Manchester, Kim Ruscoe and Christine Dando complained that they could not get a Christian act of worship for their children at Crowcroft Park Primary School. In Ealing, Mrs Denise Bell made the same complaint against Acton High School, a mixed 11–18 comprehensive. Both schools had a mixed faith composition. The difference was that Crowcroft Park judged that it could design an act of worship which was equally suitable for those of all faiths and none without applying for a 'determination' (ie exemption from Section 7 of the ERA 1988), whereas Acton High secured the same result by applying to its local Standing Advisory Council on Religious Education (SACRE).

After the parents' complaints were dismissed by their local authorities they were sent to the Secretary of State. *Twenty-three months later* Mrs Bell's complaint was dismissed. Nevertheless, the school's Chair of Governors and Ealing's Chairman of Education were informed that the local SACRE had defied the will of Parliament by granting a 'determination' to the whole school when more than 50 per cent of pupils were from a Christian background. The Minister, when pressed by PACE for action, claimed that only the courts could reverse the SACRE decision. Further pressed to bring such a court action, the Minister refused, being content with a warning to Ealing that a renewed application for the 'determination' was due in two years' time.

Ruscoe and Dando's complaint had a total settlement time of two years six months, compared with the Ealing complaint's two years eight months. These times alone must cast doubt on any concern on the part of the government for parental rights. But once again a complaint against multi-faith worship was dismissed. There was, however, some consolation. Manchester's case was based firmly on the view that other than by a 'determination' sensitive arrangements for worship could not be made on any definition of worship which regarded it as 'the reverence or veneration tended to a divine being or supernatural power'. In dismissing the parents' complaint, the Secretary of State declared that this was just the kind of definition that a court would be likely to adopt. When pressed by PACE to identify 'the being or power, regarded as supernatural or divine' being revered or venerated at

Crowcroft Park by those of all faiths and none, he replied that he did not need to discern the nature of the object of worship. PACE immediately advised the parents to seek a judicial review of this decision, on the grounds of its unreasonableness. The first application was rejected. It was ruled that Parliament had intended multi-faith worship of the type arranged at Crowcroft Park. At the time of writing no decision has been made concerning a second application.

PACE has assisted parents with complaints against multi-faith worship in Bradford, Wakefield and East Ham. Those at Bradford and Wakefield were dismissed by the Secretary of State. In both cases the parents were assisted in gaining admission to schools of their choice and no legal actions ensued.

The case of the Sherborne grammar schools

The parents of two single-sex grammar schools were helped by PACE in 1992 to seek a judicial review of the Secretary of State's decision to disallow their application for grant maintained status (for a mixed grammar school) and approve Dorset Council's plans for closure as part of a comprehensive reorganisation scheme. Previous attempts at comprehensive reorganisation had been resisted by the government. This is the only legal case in which PACE has been involved which has not succeeded.

Appeal Hearings

As Andy Stillman has already shown in Chapter 2, the Education Act 1980 was a minor landmark in the history of greater parental choice in England and Wales. Concern for parental choice had been demonstrated in the 1944 Act, at Section 76. This required the Minister and local education authorities to

> have regard to the general principle that, so far as is compatible with the provision of efficient instruction and training and the avoidance of unreasonable public expenditure, pupils are to be educated in accordance with the wishes of their parents.

This was, however, far too weak to prevent local authorities from spreading pupils evenly across the available schools and overriding parental wishes. The 1980 Act imposed a *duty* on local authorities to comply with a parent's preference for admission to a county school, unless 'compliance with the preference would prejudice the provision of efficient education or the efficient use of resources' (Section 6). For selective schools, ability or aptitude tests would also apply. The Act virtually abolished catchment areas and allowed parents to express preferences for schools outside their own authority.

The most important feature of the Act was the requirement that an authority should set up appeal committees to settle admission complaints brought by parents. Local authorities were also required to publish annually for each school full details of the admission arrangements, including the number of pupils it was intended to admit in the normal year of admission. This was known as the planned admission limit (PAL). The number of pupils admitted in the school year beginning 1979 was established as the school's 'standard number', and the Act required – at a time of falling rolls – that in the case of secondary schools no PAL should be reduced to a number which was four-fifths, or less, of the 'standard number' without the Secretary of State's approval. Primary schools had slightly different rules.

The Education Reform Act (ERA) 1988 went further. Schools had to admit up to the full standard number, and if the number actually admitted in the year before the relevant section came into force was greater than the standard number this automatically became the new standard number. Furthermore, local authorities were encouraged to admit beyond the standard number by being legally required to publish for each school an 'admission number', which was numerically equal to or greater than the standard number. Individual schools were further encouraged to admit, subject to the approval of the authority (which could be overridden by the Secretary of State), a number even greater than the admission number. The ERA made it clear that no 'prejudice' to the provision of efficient education or the efficient use of resources could arise if the number admitted did not exceed that arrived at in these calculations.

In what has come to be known as the South Glamorgan case (1984), Mr Justice Forbes ruled that an appeal committee had to reach its decision in two stages by asking first, whether there is 'prejudice', and second, if there is, whether it is sufficient to outweigh the 'parental factors'? This was an important judgment. It made it clear for the first time that there was no duty laid on an authority to avoid prejudice to the provision of efficient education or the efficient use of resources. It still, however, allowed the appeal committee to do its own very subjective balancing act if the second stage of the process proved necessary. PACE has helped a considerable number of parents to present their cases to appeal committees in what is a veritable minefield for the uninitiated.

Some Issues

The comprehensive principle

What kind of people would want to deprive parents of their right to have education for their children 'in conformity with their own religious and philosophical convictions'? What would be their motives? Two things need to be said initially about this Article of the European Convention on Human Rights (see above). First, it can only be realised if there are enough parents involved to make it economically practical – even those who can afford private schools may have to make compromises. Second, it was introduced in the aftermath of the Second World War to ensure that never again would a state be able to hold in thrall the minds of its young citizens.

One answer to the first question posed above is 'teacher organisations'. In 1970, the National Union of Teachers (NUT) Annual Conference approved proposals which claimed it would be entirely proper to limit parental choice:

> By comprehensive education ... we mean the absence of selection procedures which either directly or indirectly prevent each school from having *a representative cross-section of the full ability range* ... if legislation is to have more force than a pious hope it is necessary to limit parents' choice of school. (emphasis added)

It went on to say that parental choice should not be exercised contrary to public policy – in this case forcing children to mix with a cross-section of their contemporaries. The other teacher organisations took the same line, although not always as explicitly as the NUT.

The putative advantages of mixing pupils along ability lines can logically be extended to other social mixes. The comprehensive principle, in its most generalised educational form, is expressed thus:

> Each school, or group within a school, should contain a representative cross-section of the population at large, in respect of: socio-economic group, intelligence, race, culture, religion and gender.

It is a principle that need not be limited to education. By a suitable replacement of 'school' it can be made applicable to such elites as Parliament and to such 'negative elites' as the prison population.

The comprehensive principle can only find expression by limiting the rights of individuals. Given the *natural* inequalities of human beings, a full elimination of *social* inequalities can never lead to 'equality of results' at any stage of the educational process. All that can be guaranteed, compatible with liberty, is 'equality of opportunity'. Another reason for insisting on 'equality of opportunity' is that individuals may not all seek the same outcome.

This distinction between 'equality of opportunity' and 'equality of results' has been identified by Torsten Husen, the distinguished Swedish educationalist, as the basis of a continuing struggle in education between two philosophies – the 'liberal' versus the more 'radical' or sociological, and sometimes Marxist (Husen, 1975, p 39). It is, of course, the same struggle as that being waged between supporters of parental rights and proponents of the comprehensive principle.

Most of the court cases described have been concerned with attempts by local councils to apply the comprehensive principle: the elimination of selective schools (Sherborne); the attempt to secure racial mixes in schools (Dewsbury); the devising of a form of worship equally suitable for those of all faiths and none (Manchester and Ealing); the marginalisation of single-sex education (Merrywood); the attempt to deny parents education for their children in a traditional English and Christian environment (Dewsbury and Manchester); and the insistence on teaching a young child elements of a language and culture different from her own (Cleveland). It is significant that Cleveland's policy of not wishing to allow school transfers unless they were 'in the best interests of the pupil' (as determined, of course, by Cleveland) was in opposition to the will of Parliament, as expressed in the Education Act 1980 (Section 6(2)).

Multicultural education

A common thread in a number of these cases is the multicultural nature of the school intake. This poses a major problem for curriculum planners. The issues are complex, and need careful analysis. It goes without saying that any treatment of multicultural education which ignores parents is defective.

It is first necessary to underline the clear distinction between race and culture. The UNESCO scientists responsible for *The Race Concept* (UNESCO, 1952 and 1979) have spoken of the overriding need to define race biologically and to distinguish it from culture. As they put it, 'The long-standing confusion between race and culture has produced fertile soil for the development of racism' (1952, p 5). An individual is in no way responsible for his race, and it should never be allowed to advantage or disadvantage him. Culture, on the other hand, is directly related to the formation of the individual. PACE has fought for the rights of individuals to enjoy their own culture, but would never support parents whose preference for a school was based simply on race. It is significant that the judges in the Cleveland appeal case extracted from the CRE an admission that it was just as unacceptable to press for racially mixed schools as for racially segregated schools.

The parents helped by PACE in Dewsbury, Manchester and Cleveland have all been victims of this confused thinking which fails to make the distinction between race and culture. The so-called multicultural policies of these authorities are based on this confusion. It is not remotely racist to want one's children brought up in one's own culture. After all, Article 30 of the Convention on the Rights of the Child guarantees this very thing.

Whereas there is no direct connection between race and the curriculum, there is a very close one between culture and the curriculum. Culture may be defined (in the anthropological sense) as 'the sum total of the material and intellectual equipment whereby a people satisfy their biological and social needs and adapt themselves to the environment'. It includes such ephemeral and marginal elements as the graffiti in tube stations. This should not, however, blind us to the fact that at the heart of culture are the more substantial components vital to the people's identity and survival, such as language, religion and morals.

The school curriculum is a selection of items – from the culture of the educating community – thought worthy of being introduced to those being educated. Two questions immediately arise. Who makes the selection? And on what basis is it made? In the last analysis the answer to the first must be 'the parent' or 'the state'. The teacher has an important role in education, being a professional, well qualified to suggest the best way of taking the child from A to B. But it is not proper for the teacher to decide the value system that will determine the direction in which the child's development will take place.

These questions have special importance in multicultural Britain today. The ethnic minorities have their own cultures, as does the indigenous population. There are three major curricular options in such a society. The first – assimilation – requires children from ethnic minorities to follow the curriculum appropriate to the majority culture. When in Rome, do as the Romans do. The second – cultural diversity – respects the rights of members of all cultures to promote their own culture and have their children brought up in it. The third option – equality – requires that all children, irrespective of their cultural backgrounds and the wishes of their parents, should receive common educational experiences. For this to be more than mere tokenism, the common curriculum would have to contain contributions that are in some sense *equal* from each of the several cultures represented in the school (or in the UK, some would say). It would also have to be imposed on all. To understand the implications of these options, it is instructive to apply them to a small but very important part of the curriculum, the act of worship. Clearly the first option would deprive ethnic minorities of their rights as parents. The third option denies these rights to all communities equally. Only the second option is compatible with the rights of parents as recognised in Article 2 of Protocol No 1 of the European Convention on Human Rights.

Common school religion

The equality option is based firmly on the comprehensive principle: common experiences for all in common schools. These in turn tend to generate a common faith. This is a familiar pattern, and the subject of intense debate in the USA. Charles Glenn Jr, Massachusett's Head of Educational Equity, in *The Myth of the Common School* (1987), devotes a chapter to 'The common school as a religious institution' and follows it with 'The opposition to common school religion'. To Dewey (1934), the common school religion was a militant secularism, but later educational philosophers such as Philip Phenix subjected the religion of the common school to searching criticism. They suggested that the early ideals had not been realised and that the schools had become hotbeds of moral confusion.

It is too early to say how common school religion is developing here. Multi-faith worship, as in Manchester, has syncretistic overtones redolent of the theological teaching of Professor John Hick. On the other hand, multi-faith worship in Ealing is, according to the Education Chairman who promoted it, aimed at helping children of all faiths and none 'to appreciate the power of ideas and the way in which they have shaped the world in which we live'. There is also evidence, particularly from Manchester, of the emergence of religious relativism. The Agreed Syllabus, *Multifaith Manchester*, emphasises equal respect for all faiths as a goal for the whole curriculum. This gave rise to a second complaint by the parents about Crowcroft Park Primary School (which was also dismissed) that the school had integrated the RE and the secular curriculum in such a way that they were prevented from exercising their legal right of withdrawal.

It is remarkable that illiberal egalitarian concepts can seemingly command wide public support. It is achieved by the clever manipulation of language. The confusions between 'race' and 'culture' and between 'equality of opportunity' and 'equality of results' have already been examined. An even greater confusion surrounds the use of the term 'respect' and bedevils discussion of multicultural matters. To an educational administrator, 'respecting all faiths equally' amounts to no more than making available minority faith schools on the same basis as Christian schools, or providing opportunities for minority faith worship alongside Christian worship in county schools. This is an essential requirement for the liberal educator concerned with equality of opportunity. It is as far removed as it could be from the notion of an educator upholding the principle that all faiths are equally worthy of respect and teaching this to young children as an article of faith (as in Manchester). An even greater misunderstanding is possible. This results from the failure to distinguish between respect for a person's religion or belief system and his right to adopt and profess it. A distinction which is easily discerned in a political context goes unrecognised here. Try asking a socialist if he respects Thatcherism, or vice versa! There is absolutely no reason why anybody should be expected to support the views of others provided he supports their right to hold them. Only moral relativists could think otherwise (see Naylor, 1991, for a fuller treatment of this issue).

Conclusions

The best fillip for parental rights came with the legislation designed to prevent local authorities from diverting pupils from popular to unpopular schools. Unfortunately, heightened parental expectations cannot be fulfilled once a school is full to capacity.

Opting-out has given parents the opportunity to remove schools from council control, but parents cannot command a majority on their governing bodies. These schools, in time, should offer greater diversity. The government, however, is leaving too much to the parents; and there is also a danger that the new Funding Agencies will assume some of the powers of the old education authorities. A tighter curb on diversity comes from the centrally imposed National Curriculum.

Recent legal actions have shown that some local authorities are heavily committed to using schools for social engineering. Attempts to secure common experiences for all children and to jettison the liberal concept of equality of opportunity for the more radical and sociological one of equality of outcome demonstrate contempt for individual rights.

The determined attempts to dislodge the traditional religions as sources of inspiration for our pupils have brought Christians and Muslims closer together. The present government, however, has not adequately supported the right to Christian worship. The law may need amendment, but it is doubtful whether an administration displaying increasing signs of corporatism will act.

The rights of parents to have education for their children in conformity with their own religious and philosophical convictions are set out in the European Convention. This has been ratified by successive UK governments since 1952, but none has made it a bedrock of its public educational policy. PACE has canvassed all the main political parties on their support for Article 2. Only the Labour Party has failed to endorse it. The Conservative government's White Paper of 1985, *Better Schools*, made it plain, however, that it was only going to apply to the independent sector.

English law is basically weak on curricular freedom for parents. The subversive nature of the new concepts of equality – encouraged by the Organisation for Economic Cooperation and Development (OECD) – make it imperative that the European Convention is incorporated into English law. The impending crisis in education may force the government's hand. It is only by developing a diversity of schooling that offers distinctive approaches to the common goals essential to our society that we can rebuild broad support for public education.

Note

The views expressed are those of the author, and not necessarily those of PACE.

References

Dewey J (1934) *A Common Faith* Oxford, Oxford University Press.

Glenn C (1987) *The Myth of the Common School* Amherst, MA, University of Massachusetts Press.

Husen T (1975) *Social Influences on Educational Attainment* Paris, OECD.

Jackson B (1964) *Streaming; An Education System in Miniature* London, Routledge & Kegan Paul.

Naylor, F (1981) *Crisis in the Sixth Form* London, Centre for Policy Studies.

Naylor F (1989) *Dewsbury: The School above the Pub* London, Claridge Press.

Naylor, F (1991) 'Freedom and respect in a multicultural society' *Journal of Applied Philosophy*, 8, 2, pp 225–230.

UNESCO (1952) *The Race Concept* Paris, UNESCO.

UNESCO (1979) *Declaration on Race and Racial Prejudice* Paris, UNESCO.

Index